T0244452

TASCHEN PRESENTS

A FILM BY

NICOLAS ROEG

# DAVID BOWIE

IN

TH

WHO

TO EAR

TASCHEN

PHOTOGRAPHY BY

DAVID JAMES

EDITED BY

PAUL DUNCAN

IN COLLABORATION WITH STUDIOCANAL

I'M BRITISH
I HAVE A
PASSPORT

Thomas Jerome Newton (David Bowie) arrives in Haneyville.

David Bowie being directed by Nicolas Roeg. Bowie: "I couldn't have worked with a director unless it was somebody I knew instinctively would become a mentor. I couldn't have worked with someone I considered to be less than myself—and I have a very, very high opinion of my own abilities. Within the first hour on the set, I knew that I'd picked the right one."

Hamm's

TRINI and HELEN
TRINI'S BAR Lounge
OPEN 8 AM til MIDNIGHT
Fast WINDOW

CLOSED

**David Bowie: "Working with Nicolas was one of the more important experiences that I've ever had. He has a depth, and a quality as a human being that I admire—and tried to wallow in as much as possible."**

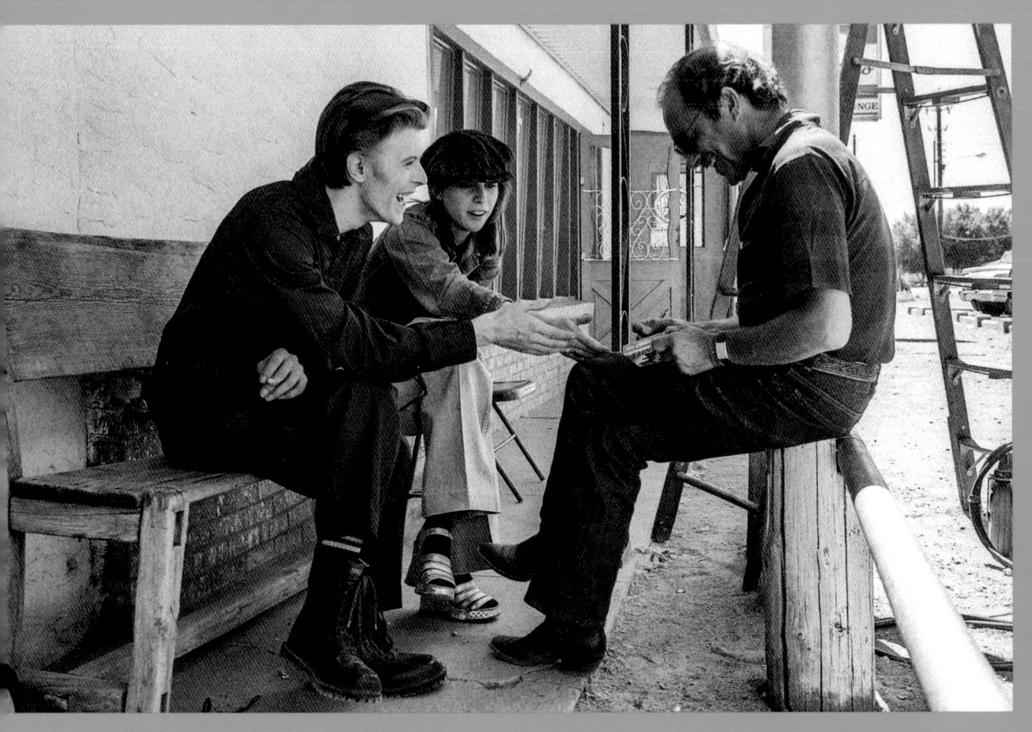

David James: "Nic was always relaxed. It was a relaxed set and everybody was having fun. Filmmaking is fun. It's supposed to be."

TRINI
TRINI'S
8 AM

milk

ZOOM
LENS

Newton falls to Earth into water, and treats water with reverence. He rapidly acquires cash through the sale of gold rings.

YOU HAVE
NINE BASIC
PATENTS HERE

Patents lawyer Oliver Farnsworth (Buck Henry) agrees to represent Newton and to form World Enterprises. Buck Henry: "It was great fun to wear those glasses that I couldn't see anything through. After the first few days of shooting my legs were a mass of sores from running into tables and chairs."

David Bowie: "We carry the luggage of otherness with us wherever we go."

**Dr. Nathan Bryce (Rip Torn), a professor of chemical engineering at a midwestern university. Bryce has reached a crisis in his career—bored with his work, separated from his wife, he distracts himself by seducing his female students.**

n who Fell to Earth"

Screenwriter Paul Mayersberg: "I've always been very interested in Japanese culture since my school days, when I saw the films of [Akira] Kurosawa and [Yasujiro] Ozu. Part of Japanese culture is quiet, contemplative, and spiritual even, while another part is bloodletting perversion. I wanted to have that comparison because it defined for me two kinds of love. It struck me that this curious coexistence of attitudes to the flesh and the spirit was perfect for our film."

**Mayersberg: "I had envisaged Bryce as a kind of playboy. A cocksman, but smooth. A smooth operator slickly worming his way into the company. We had the idea that Dr. Bryce may be played by James Coburn. I don't know how far Nic got with that but we certainly couldn't afford James Coburn." Rip Torn was cast as Nathan Bryce. "Rip Torn was a completely new idea. Here was a tense, voluble kind of man, so I began to change the lines to fit Rip."**

One of Newton's products, a self-developing 35 mm film, excites Bryce's interest, and he becomes obsessed with discovering its secret.

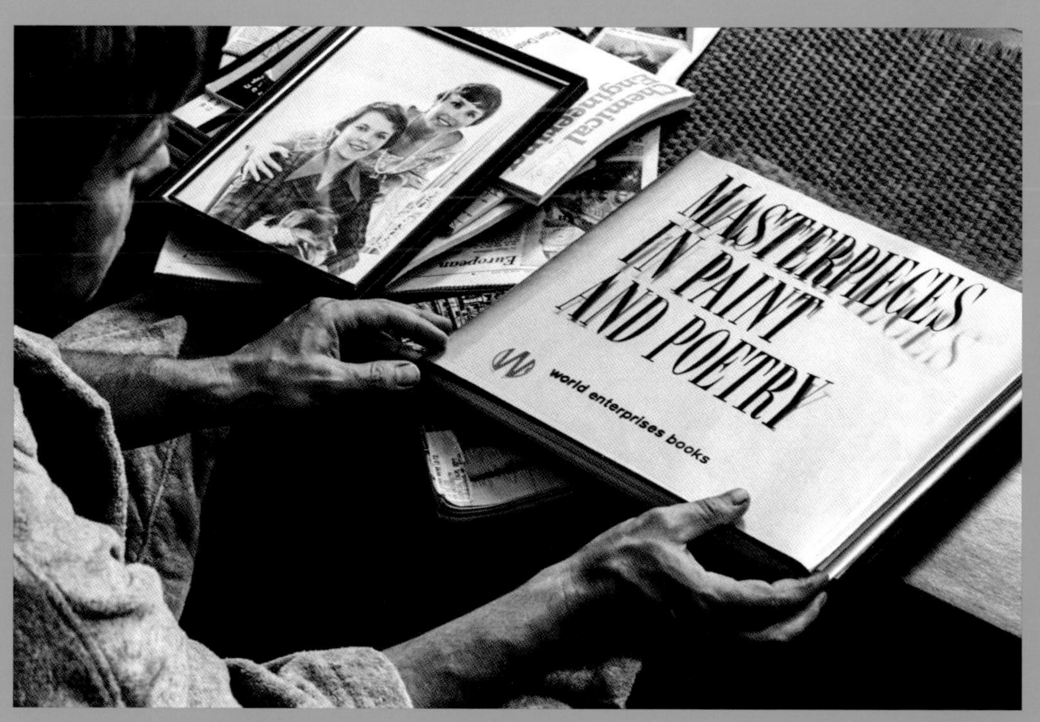


**Bryce receives a book containing the painting *Landscape with the Fall of Icarus*, as well as W. H. Auden's poem about it. Mayersberg: "In the painting no one notices the fall of Icarus, which is what Auden observed and is the basis of the poem."**

Bryce quits his post to pursue his quest.

Newton stays in the Hotel Artesia,
near the Mexican border. Bowie:
"The weight of the sky in Artesia
is something indescribable.
It's a magic place, New Mexico."

HOTEL
ARTESIA
STAURANT
BETHLEHEM
GAS-LESS

CAFE

158-ZBB

RAIL
CROSSING
ROAD
2
TRACKS
ARTESIA ALFALF
ASSOCIA
W

Lounge
FALLOUT SHELTER

Cocktail Loung

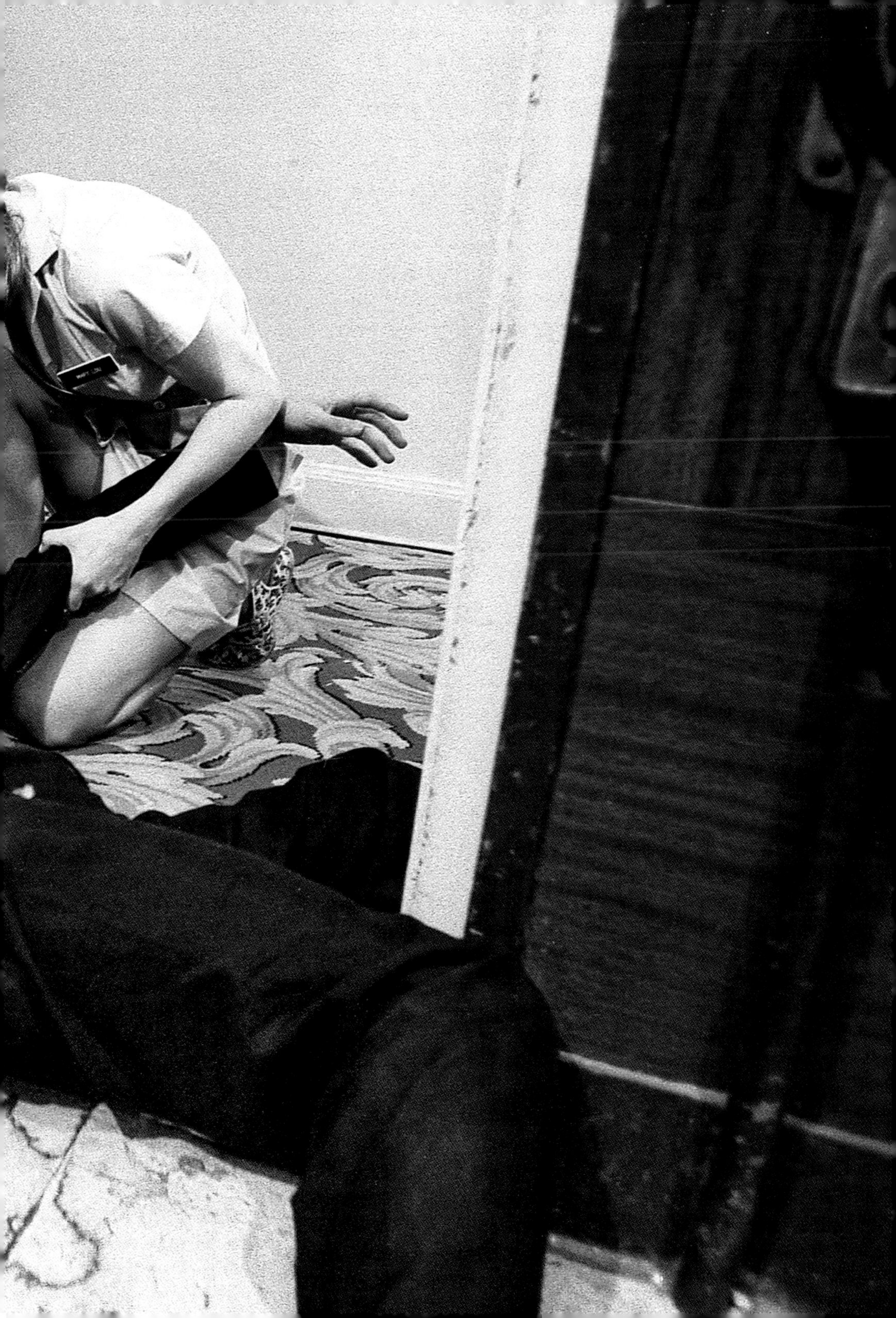

**Newton's hollow bones and weak body find it difficult to navigate the speed and gravity of life on Earth. He is aided by Mary-Lou (Candy Clark).**

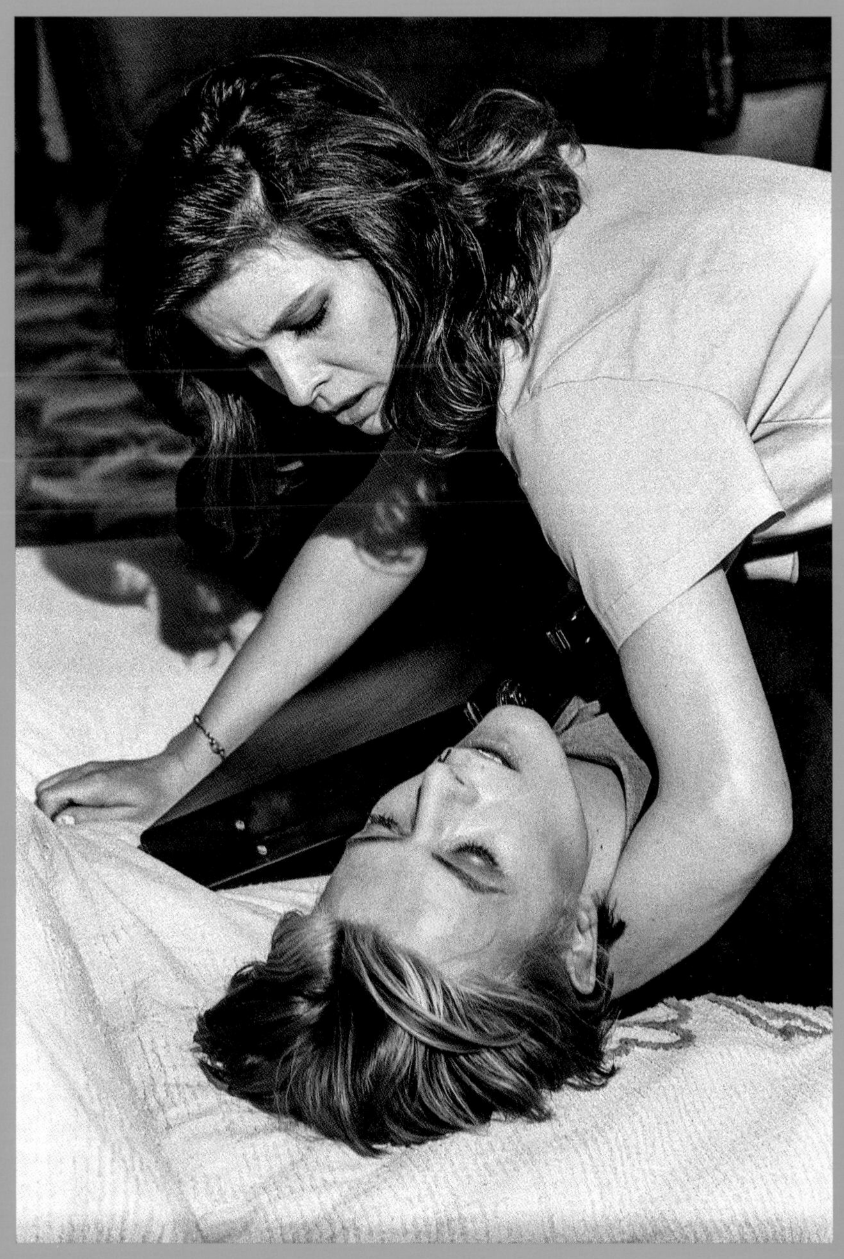

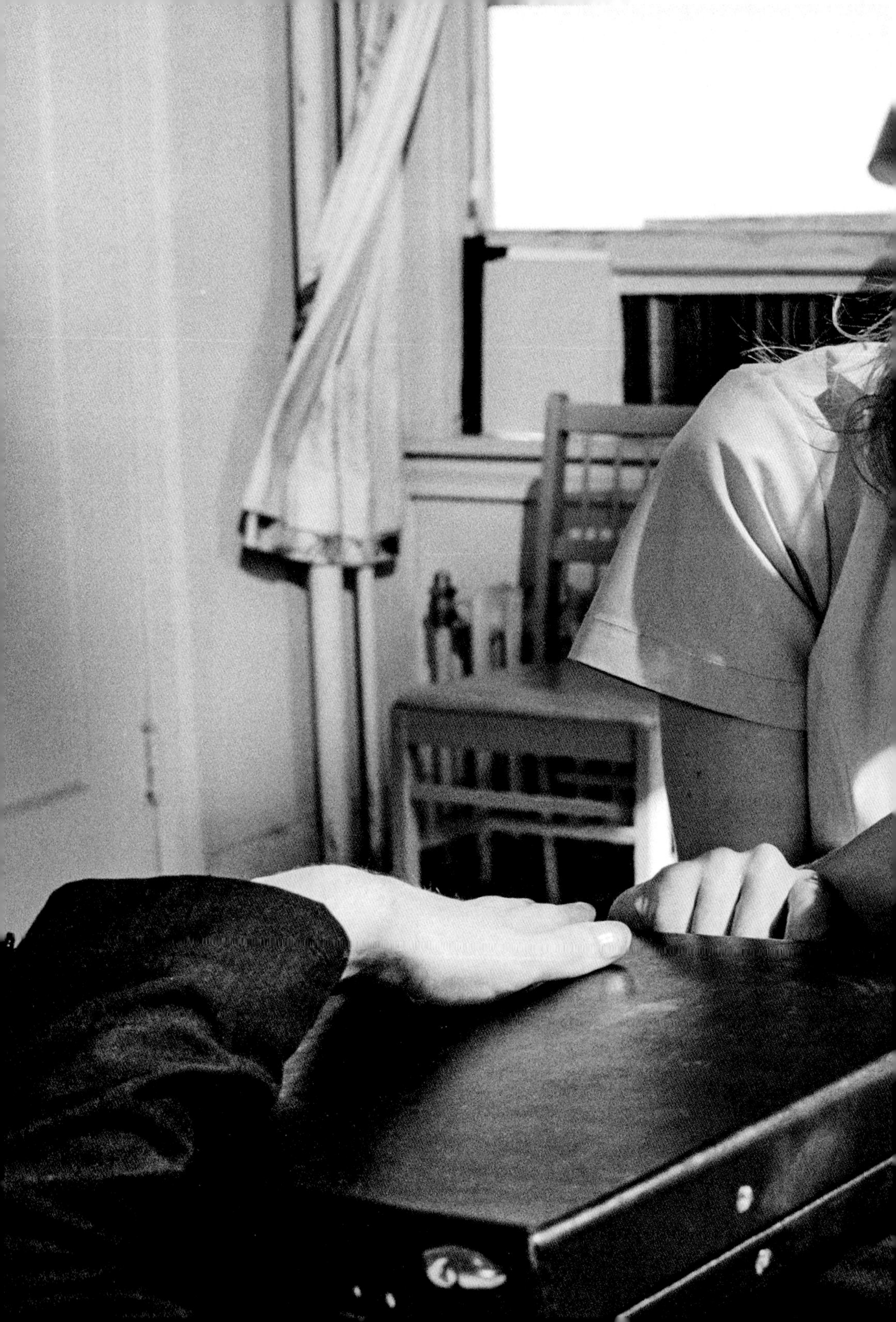

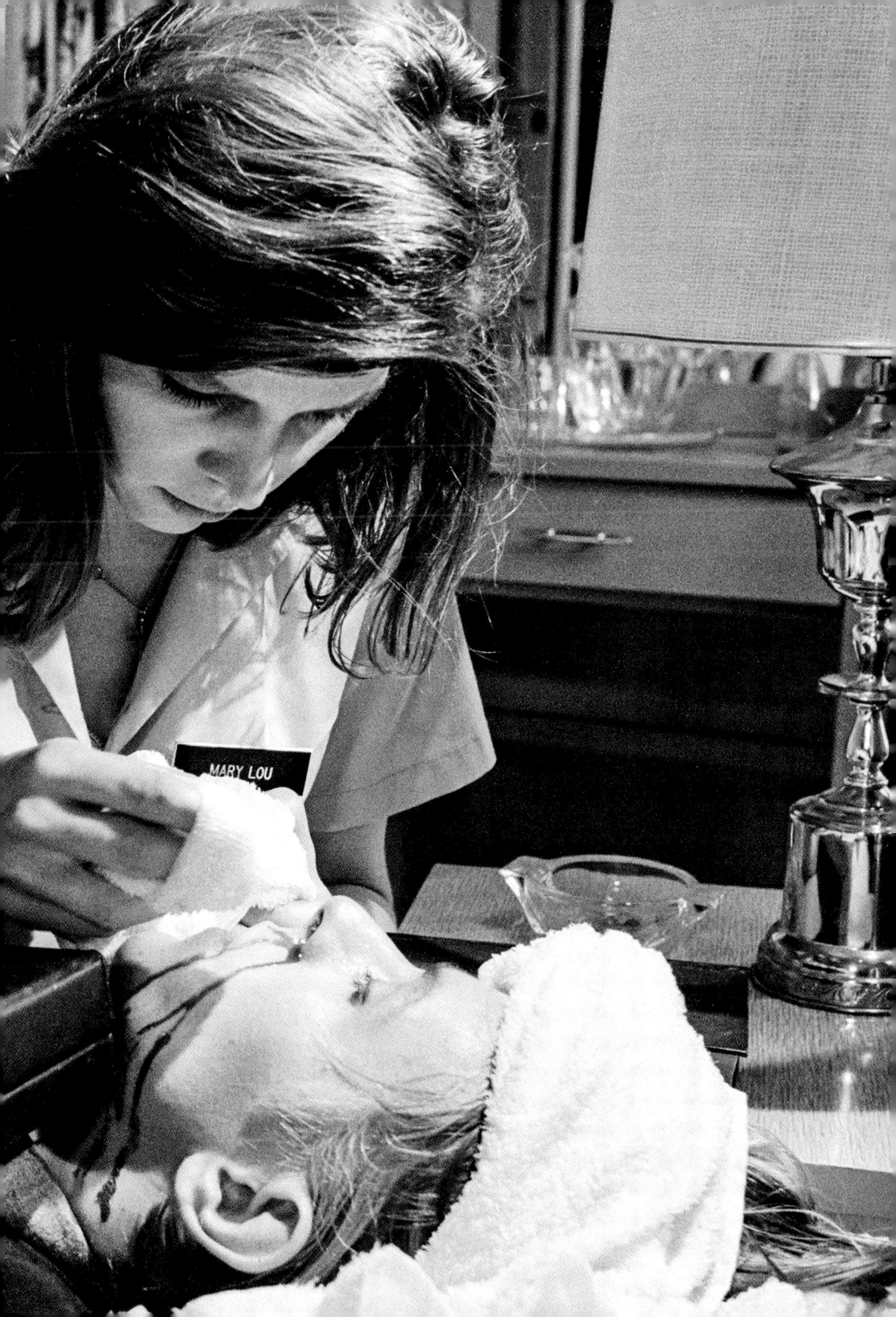
MARY LOU

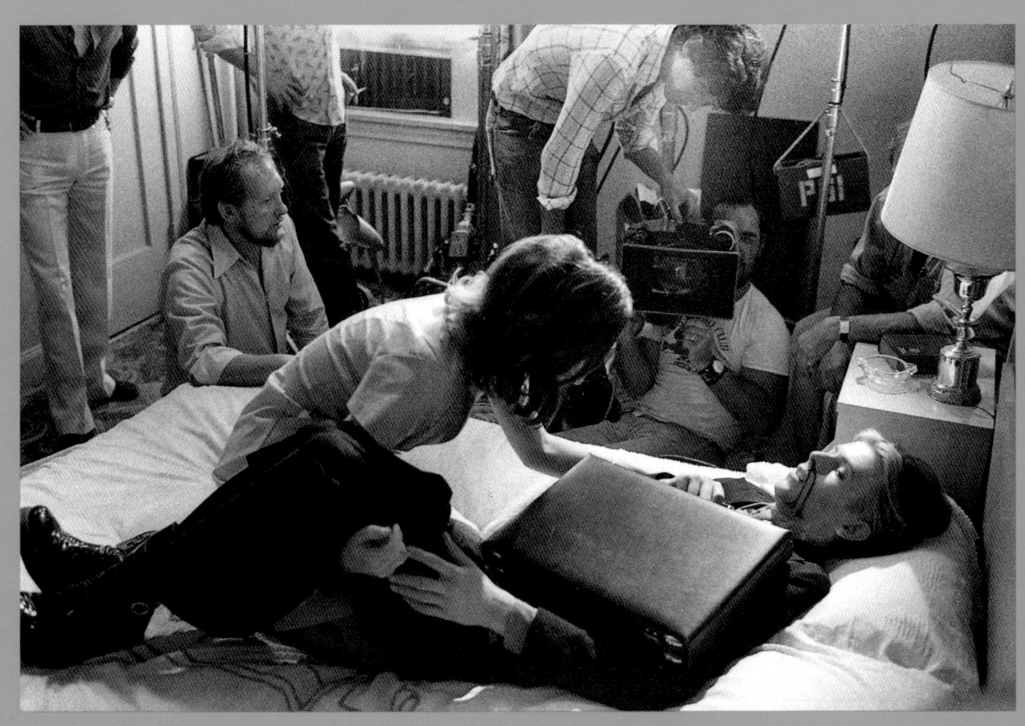

Bowie: "My preparation in those days was akin to just putting a hat on. If it looked right then that was it. I think possibly if I do generate a feeling of Newton successfully, it is only because of the deconstruction that Nic was able to perform on the basic material that I brought to the role. I was quite plastic in that way. It was easy for Nic to guide me into any area that he wanted to, like the good alchemist that he is."

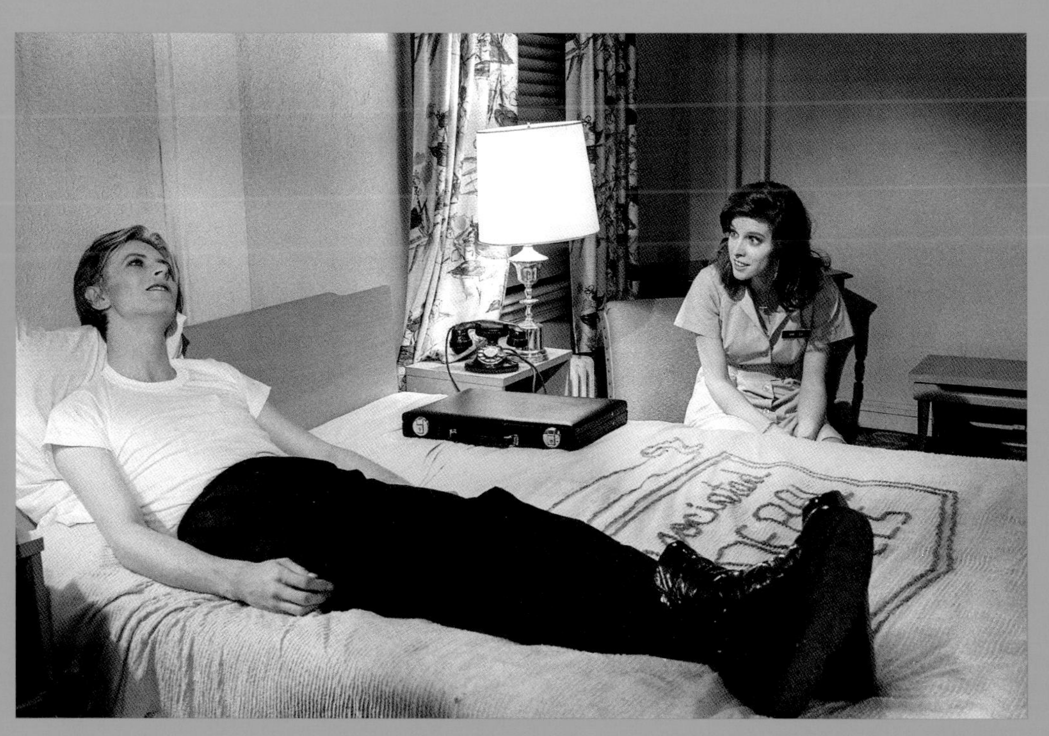

HOLY BIBLE

BEEFEATER

BOY, YOU'RE REALLY HOOKED ON WATER, AREN'T YOU?

GAS-LESS

HOTEL ARTESIA
MILLER VAN LINES
ALBUQUERQUE, NEW MEX.
Land of Enchantment

Newton moves into Mary-Lou's apartment, where he begins to fuel his addictions.

V.T.C
COCKTAIL LOUNGE

MISS CLAIROL

**Candy Clark: "David loved to run dialogue, which was a key component of how I needed to work. We'd run it backwards and forwards. He wanted to get it perfect. We'd wrap a scene and instead of going off to rest, we'd start running dialogue on the next scene that was coming up while the crew was setting up the shot. And the dialogue in this film was so good, none of us wanted to improvise a word."**

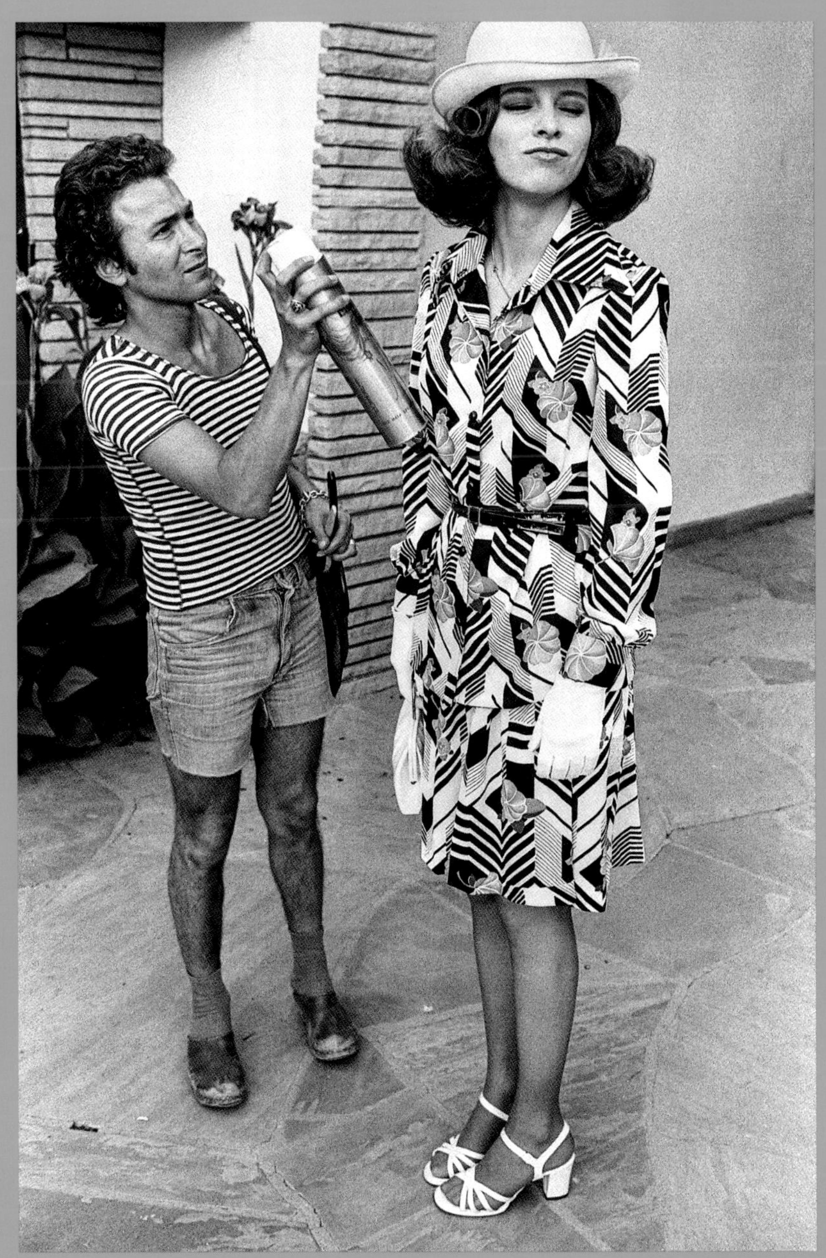

**Tommy settles into a domesticated life with Mary-Lou, always conscious of and concerned for his other family.**

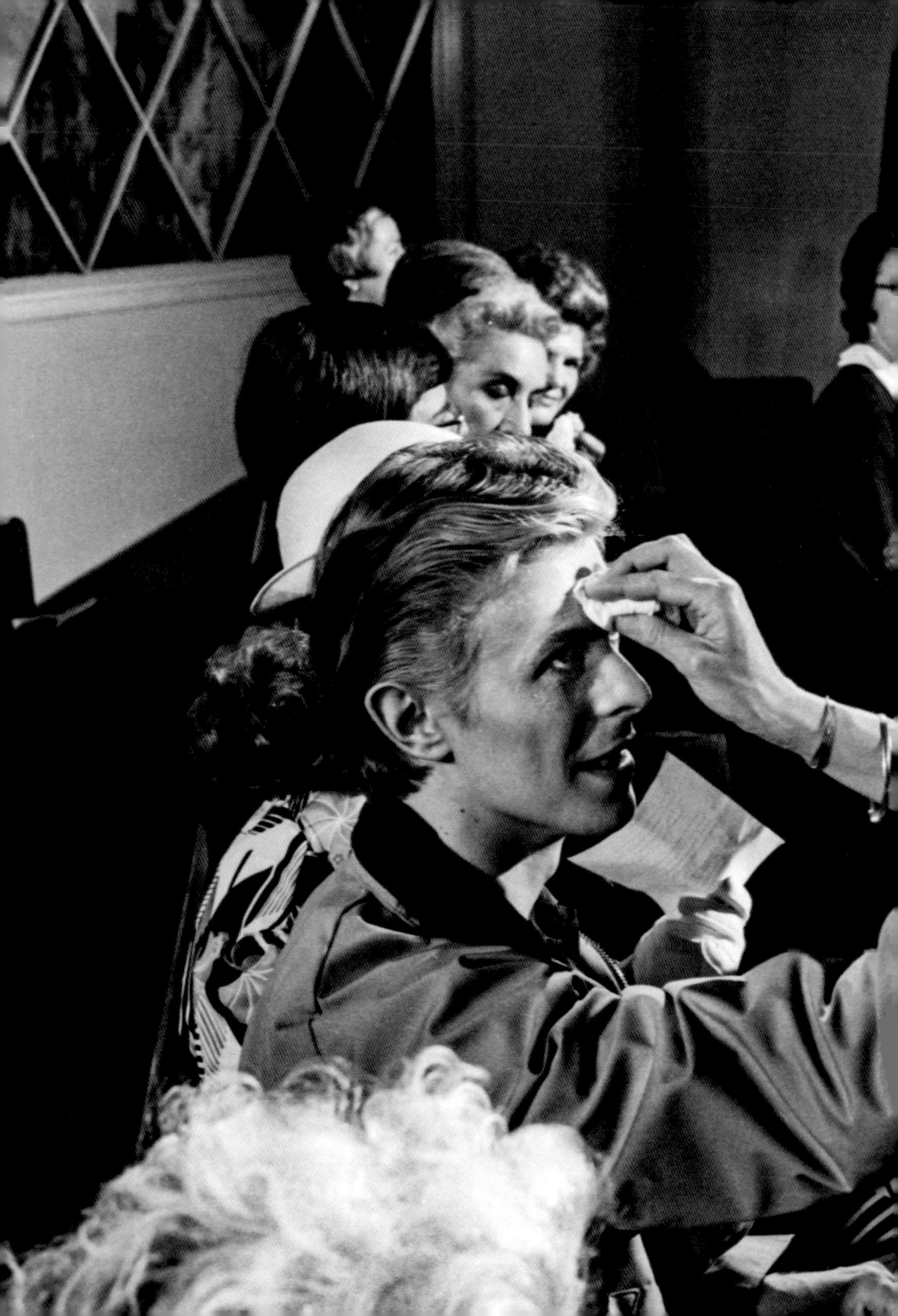

PSI MINI MOBILE FILM VAN
PRODUCTION SYSTEMS, INC.

158-ZBB
NEW YORK

Nicolas Roeg: "My interest in film is in the grammar of films, of shifting images, not relying solely on accepted practice...to use the juxtaposition of scenes to heighten the tension. It is a tension only cinema can do."

**Newton finds the place where he first fell and decides to build a house there.**

**Farnsworth to his partner, Trevor (Rick Riccardo): "Starting tomorrow we are embarking on some sort of space program."**

W

Bryce, now part of World Enterprises, is flown in to work on the space program.

**The production erected a fake Japanese-style house by the lake.**

PRODUCTION
YSTEMS, I
CA. 469-

Roeg: "I was conscious not to disturb [David] at all. There were certain people who were concerned about his unconventionality as an actor, wondering if he was being used as some sort of gimmick. Some executives even suggested post-synching another voice over Bowie's. I just said, 'Are you mad? His voice is it!' Every time someone mentioned how curious his delivery was, it pleased me more and more."

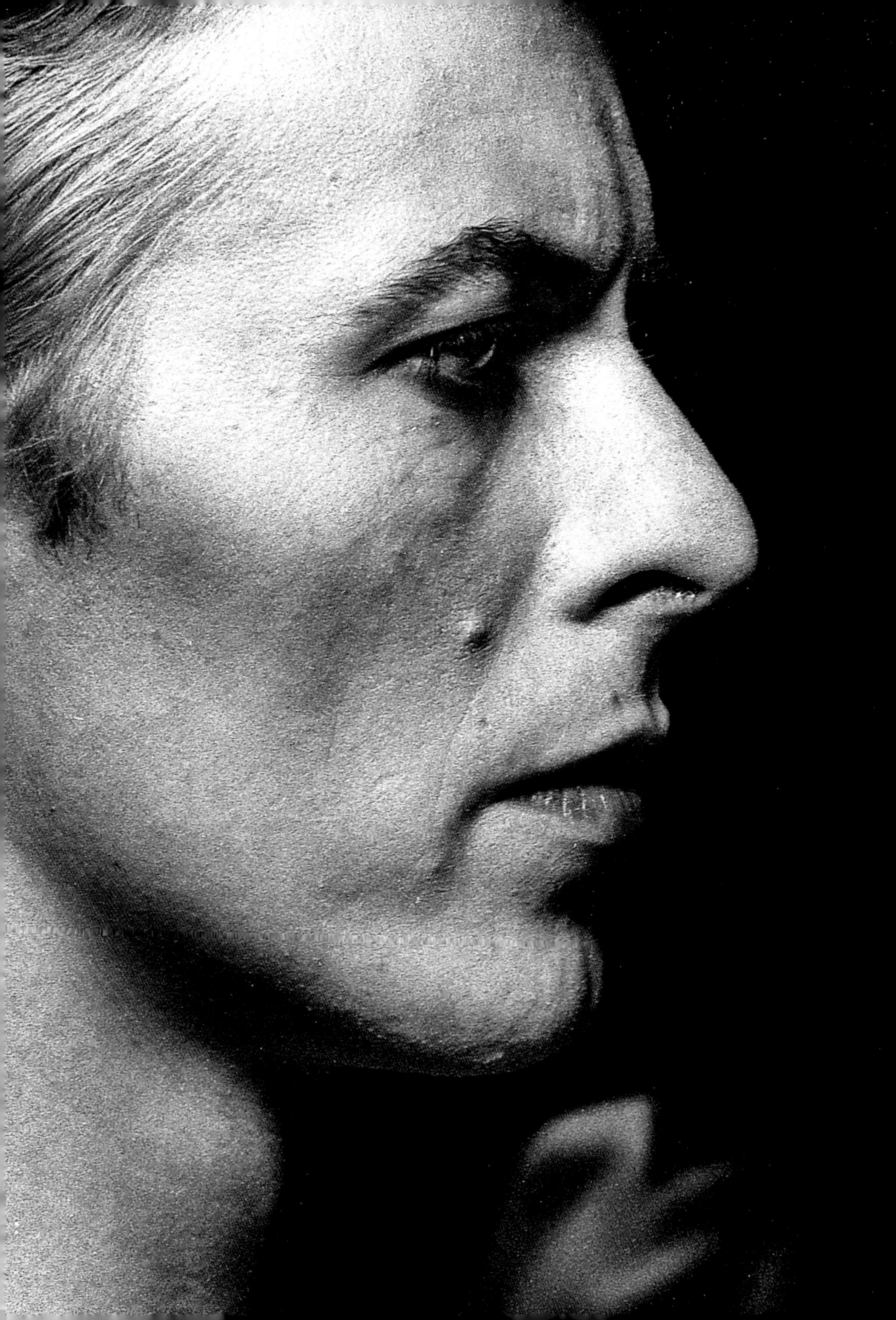

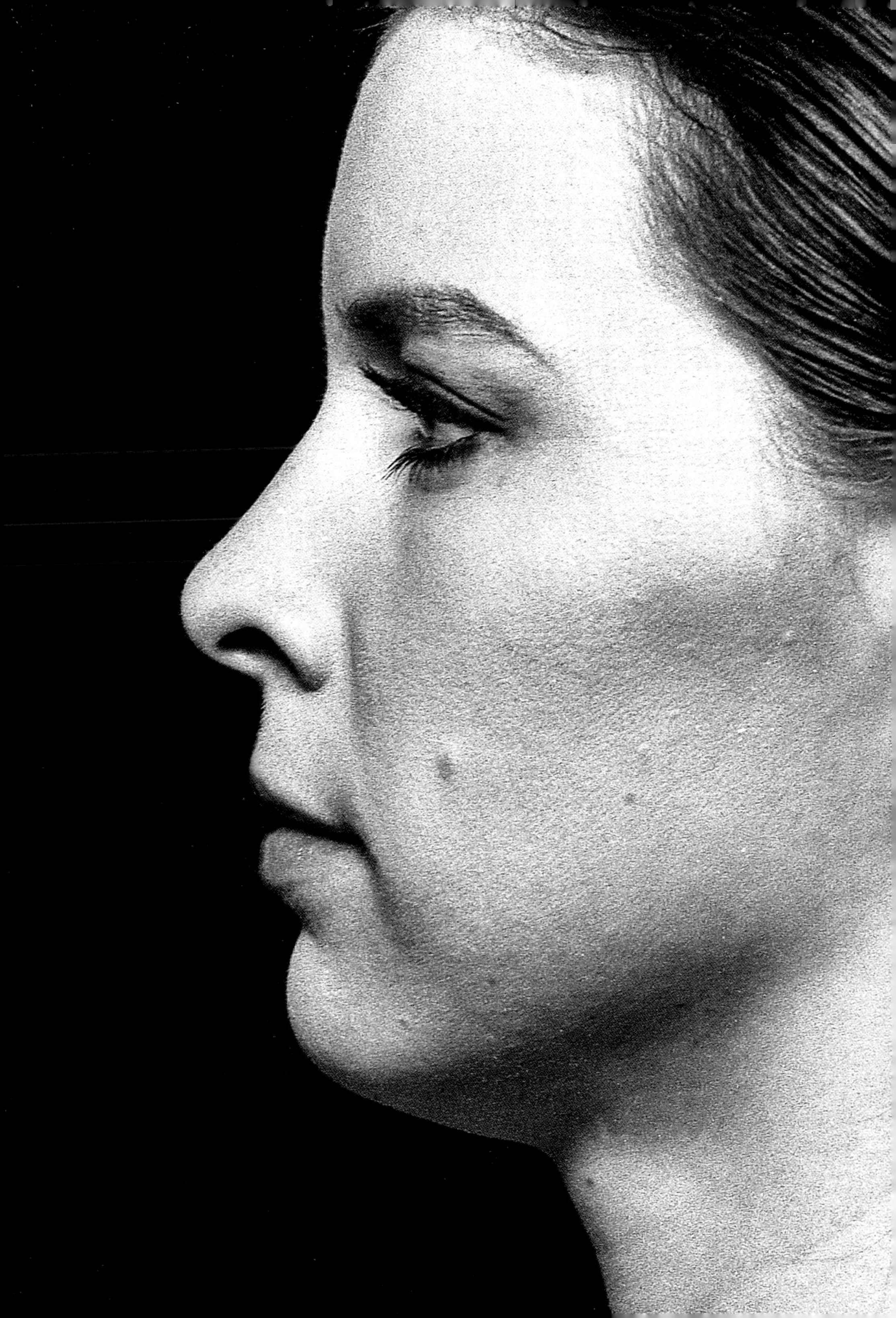

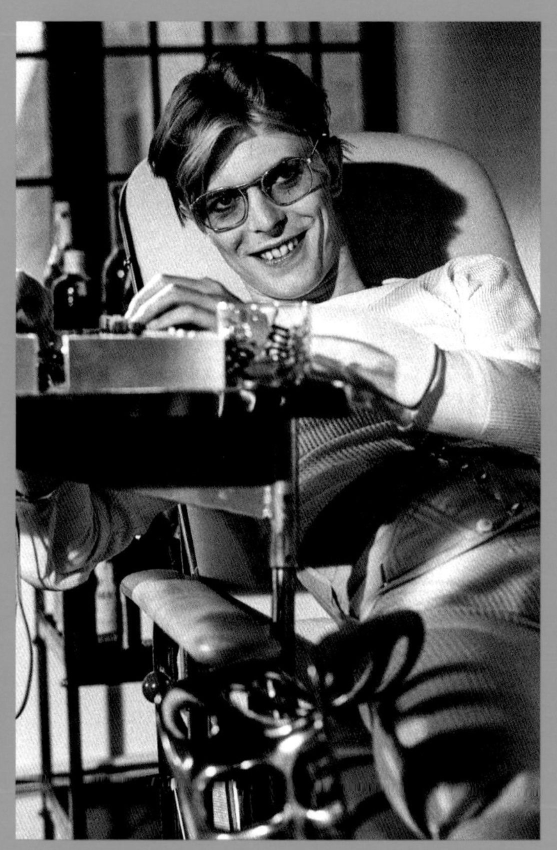

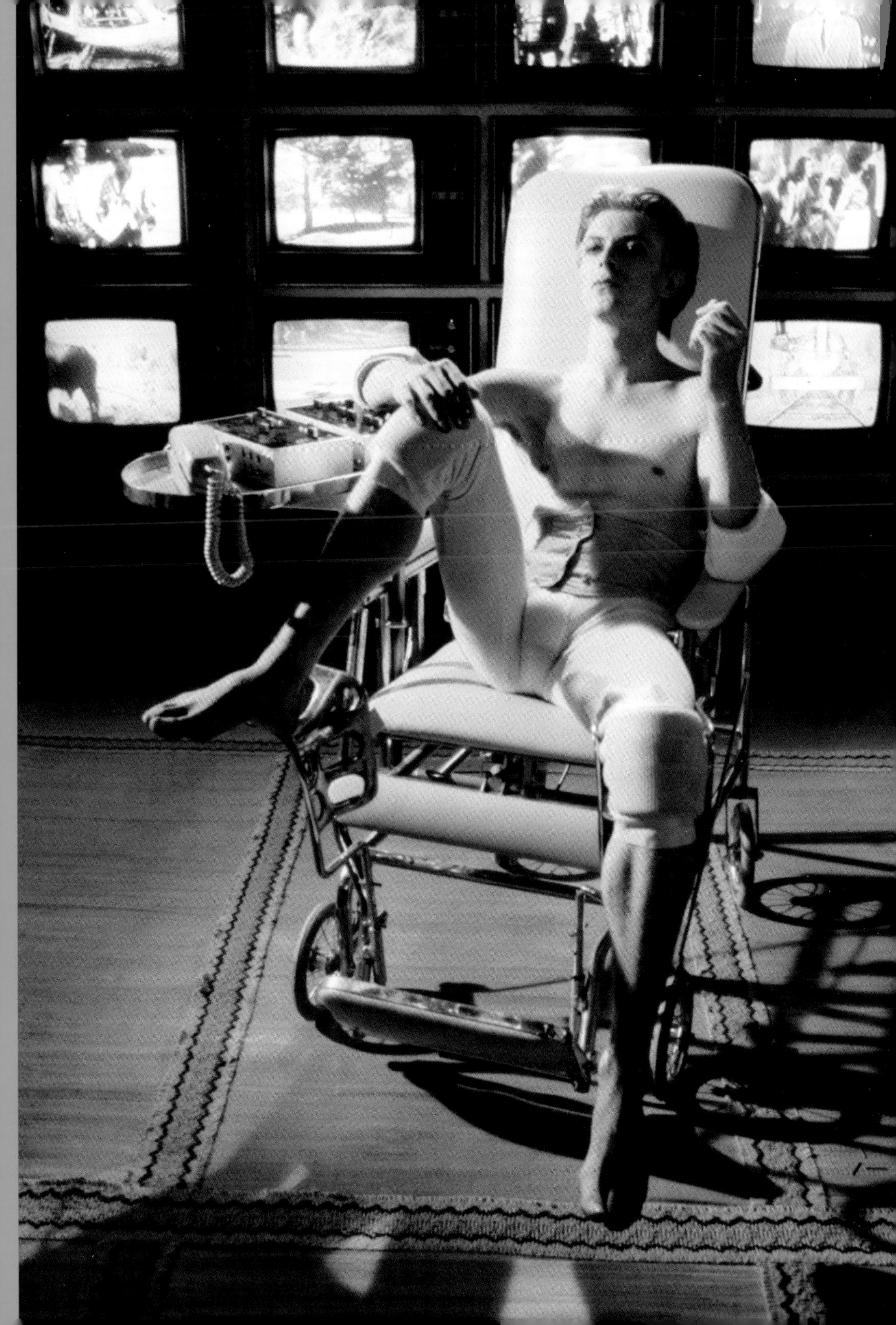

TOMMY,
WHAT'S
HAPPENED
TO YOU?

Bowie: "One of the things that Nic identified with me was that I was definitely living in two separate worlds at the same time. My state of mind was quite fractured and fragmented, but I didn't really have much emotive force going for me, so it was quite easy for me not to relate too well with others around me."

**Newton shows Bryce the spaceship. Roeg: "It is a science fiction film; science fiction without hardware. We haven't got a dial in it. No dials!"**

PANAFLEX

James: "Bowie was approachable and nice. Very down-to-earth."

Peters (Bernie Casey) tries to nego-
tiate a deal with Farnsworth but it
becomes clear that World Enterprises
is about to undergo a hostile takeover.

CHURCH OF RELIGIOUS SCIENCE

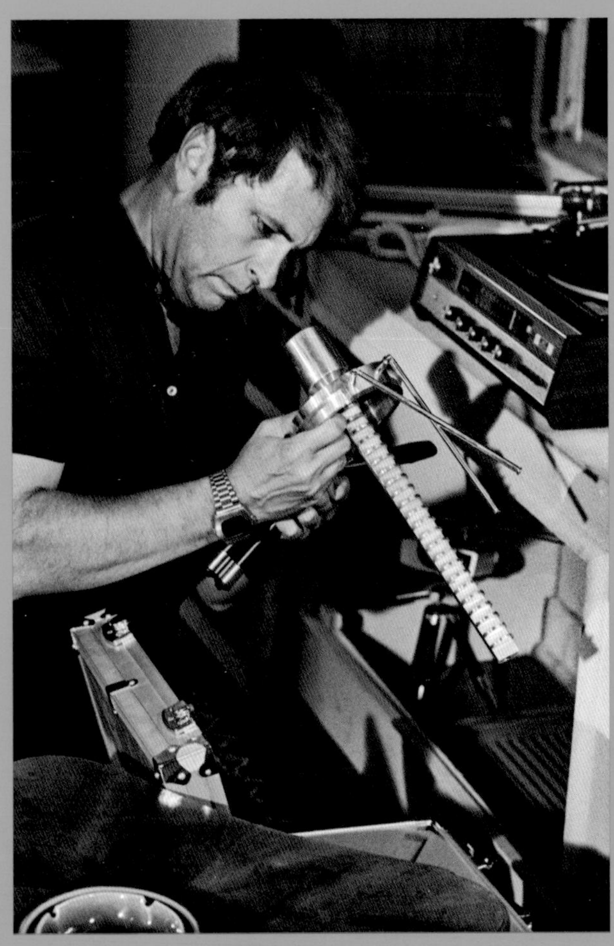

**Bryce uses his friendship to secretly take an X-ray of Newton.**

World Enterprises has stimulated the economy too much with its technological advances, so Williams (Peter Prouse) and Peters must do something about it.

Dash

**Bowie: "There are all kinds of aspects of the film that I find quite contemporary. The alcohol being one of the major stars of the movie. The degradation and destruction that it can bring to certain relationships is made very clear, if you want to read it that way."**

D.B.
RT. CC. BH.

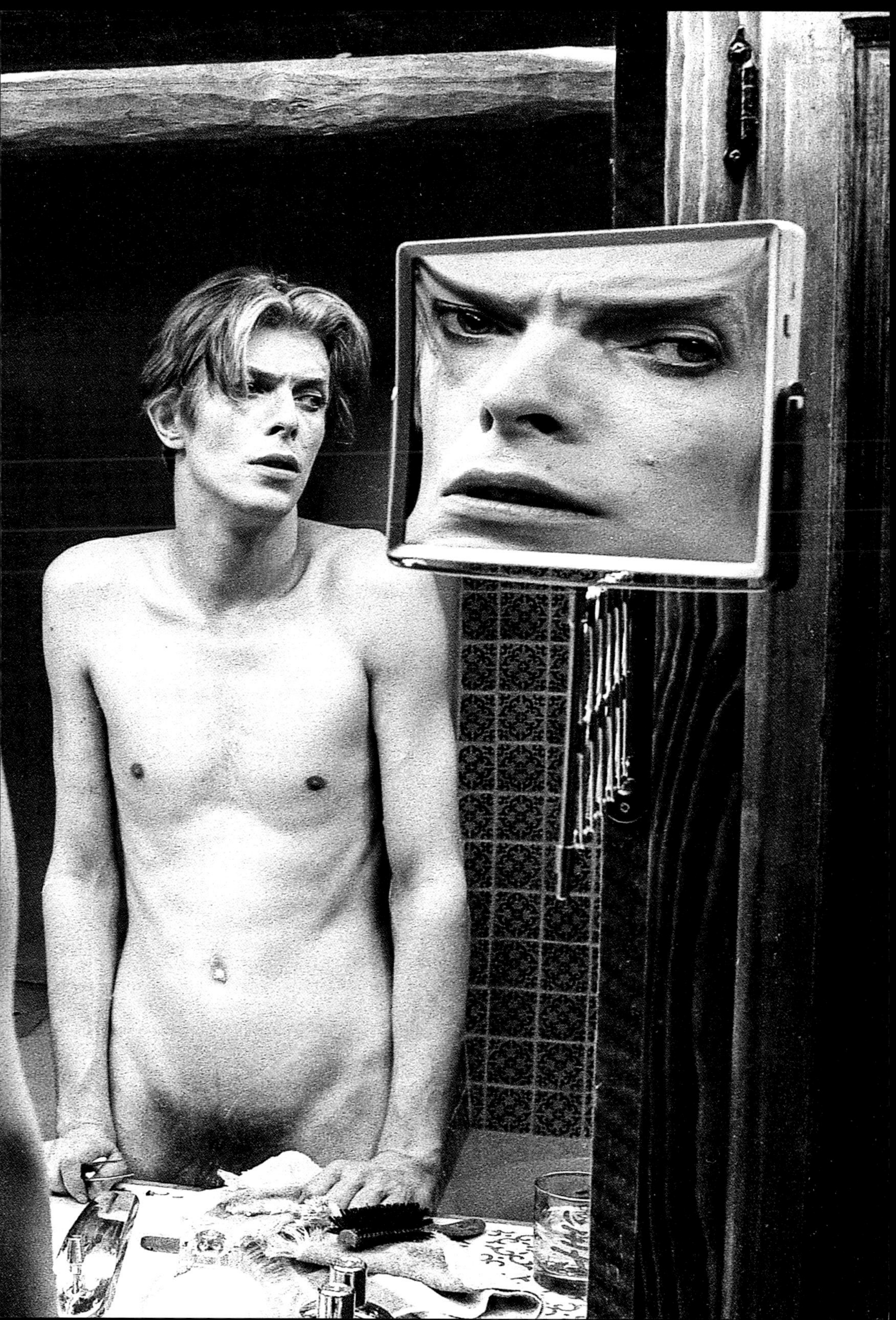

Newton makes his true feelings, and his true nature, known to Mary-Lou.

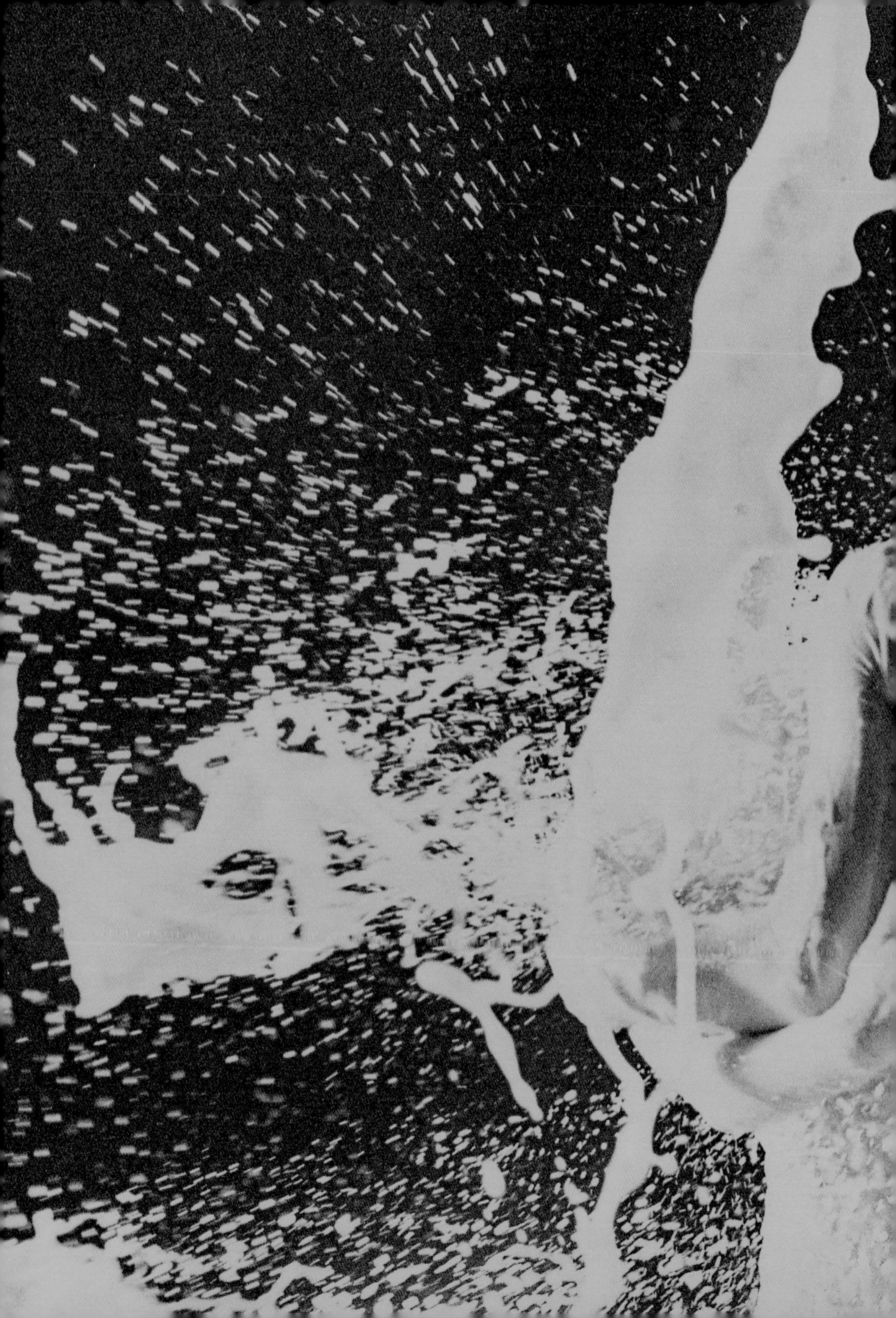

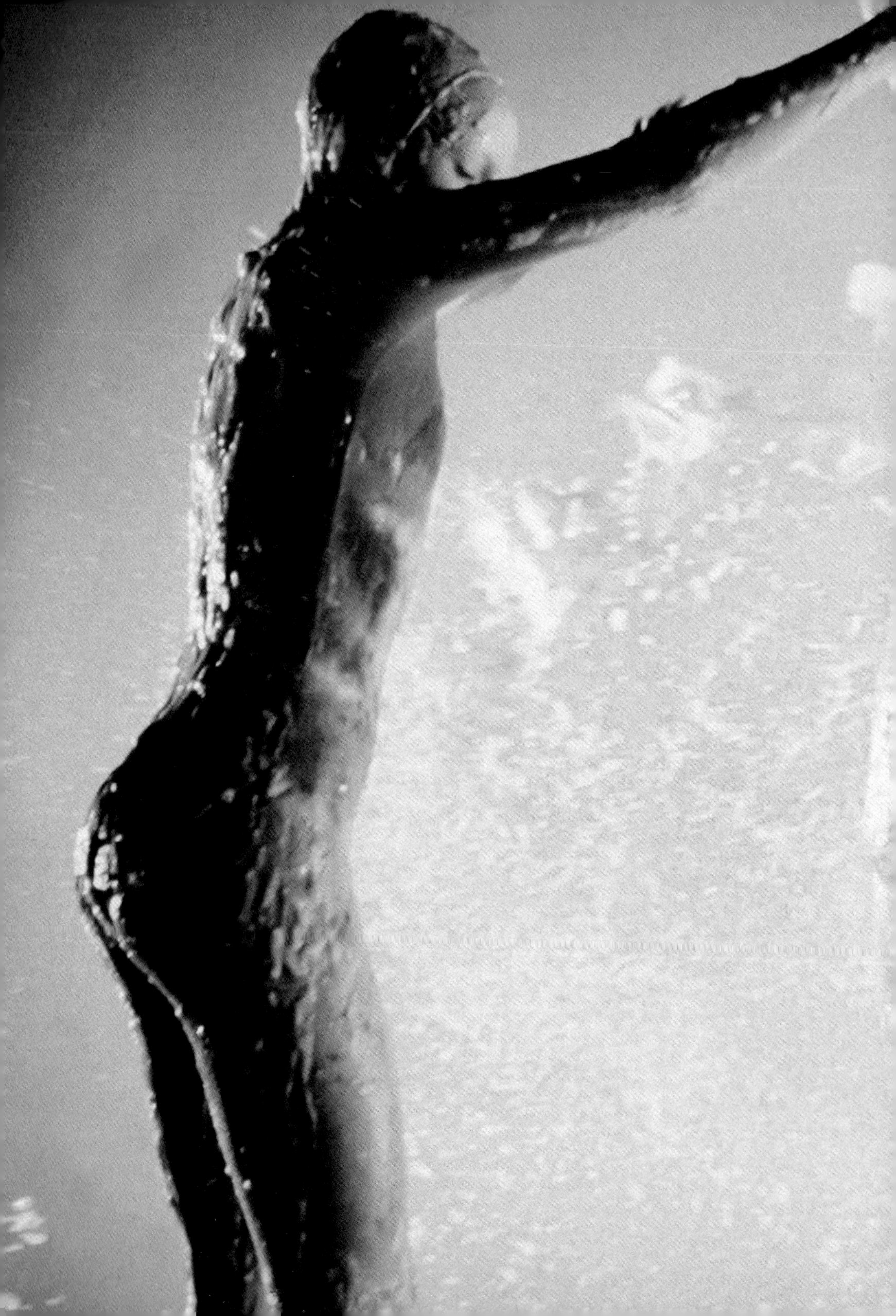

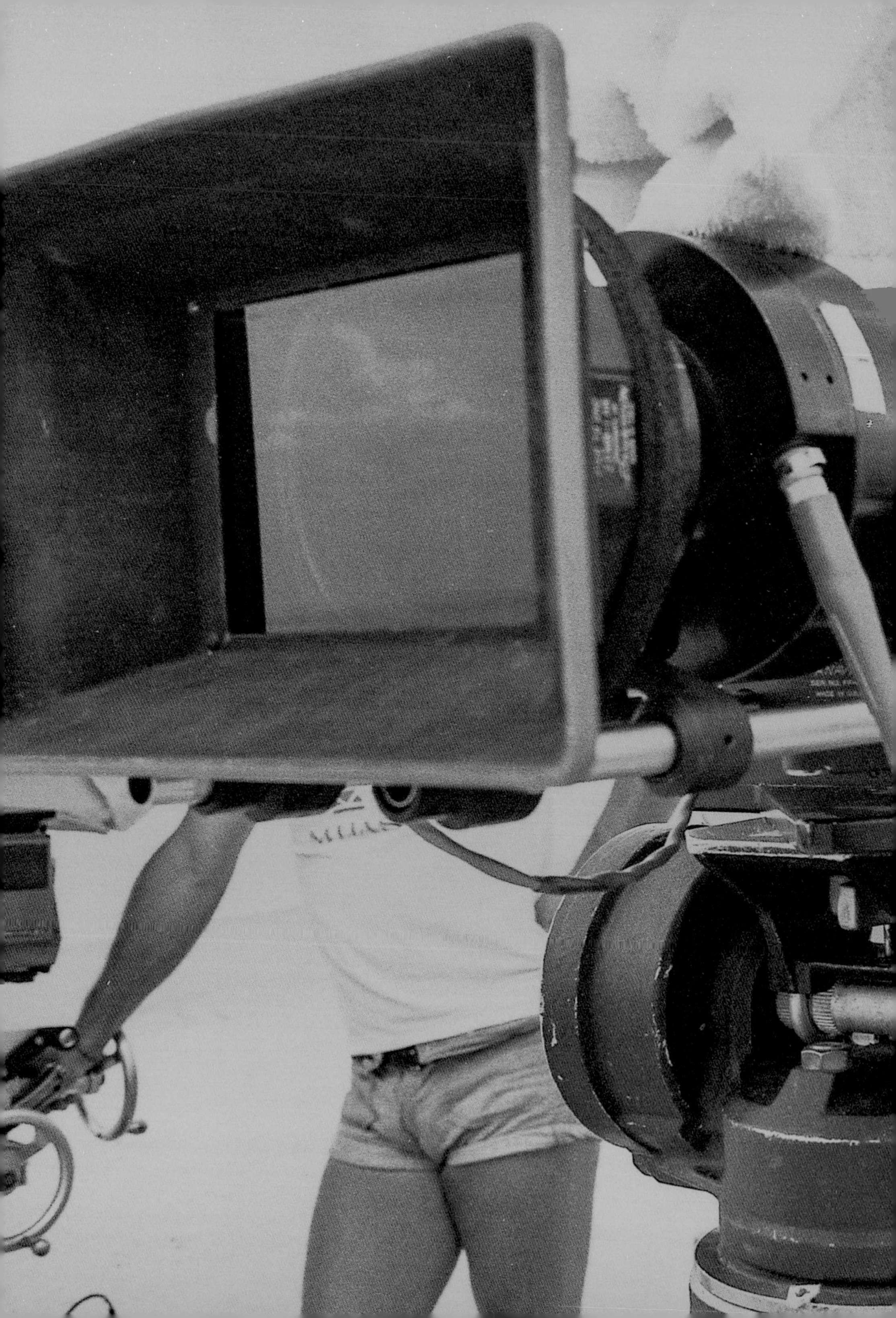

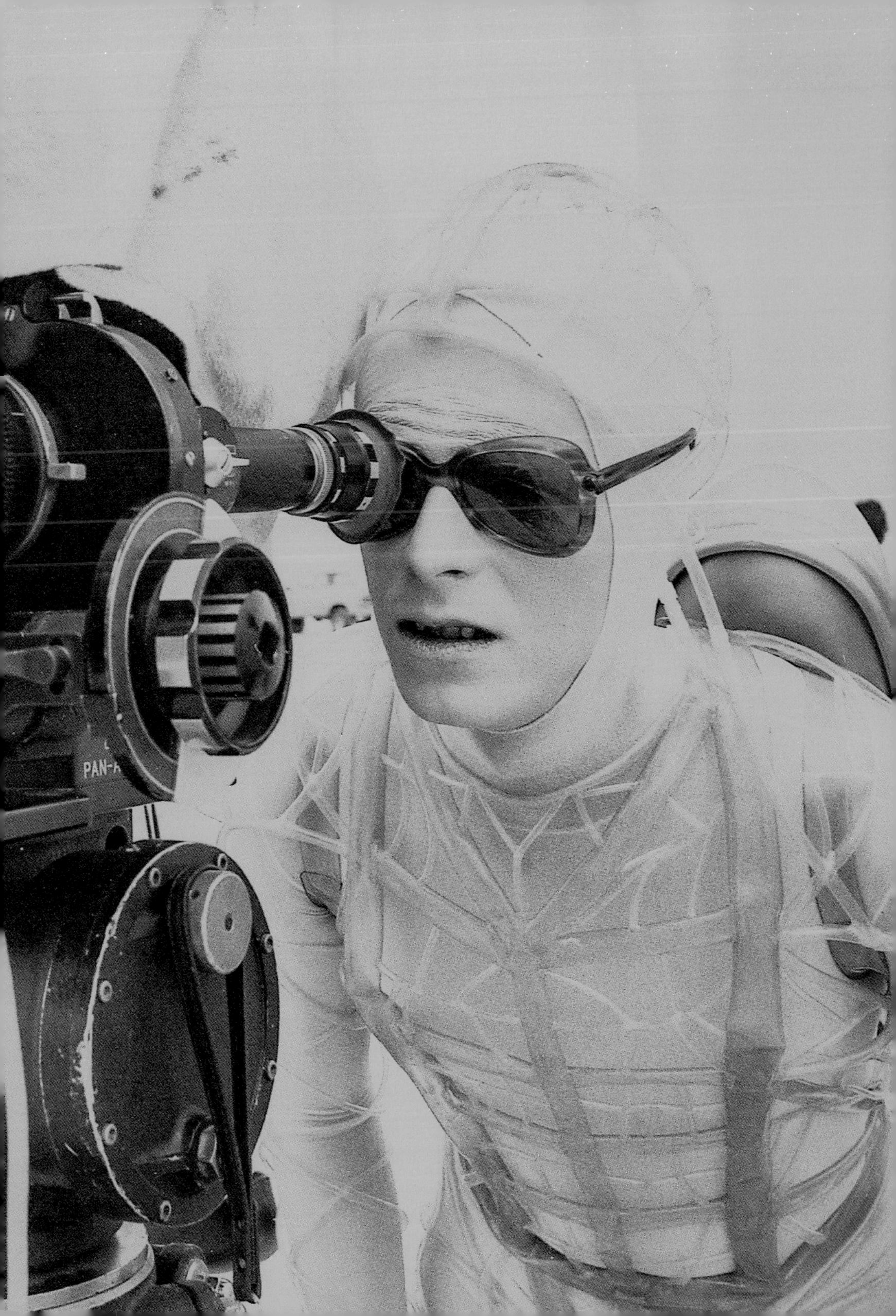

After being rejected by Mary-Lou, Newton dreams of the family he left behind on another planet, and a wife that resembles Mary-Lou.

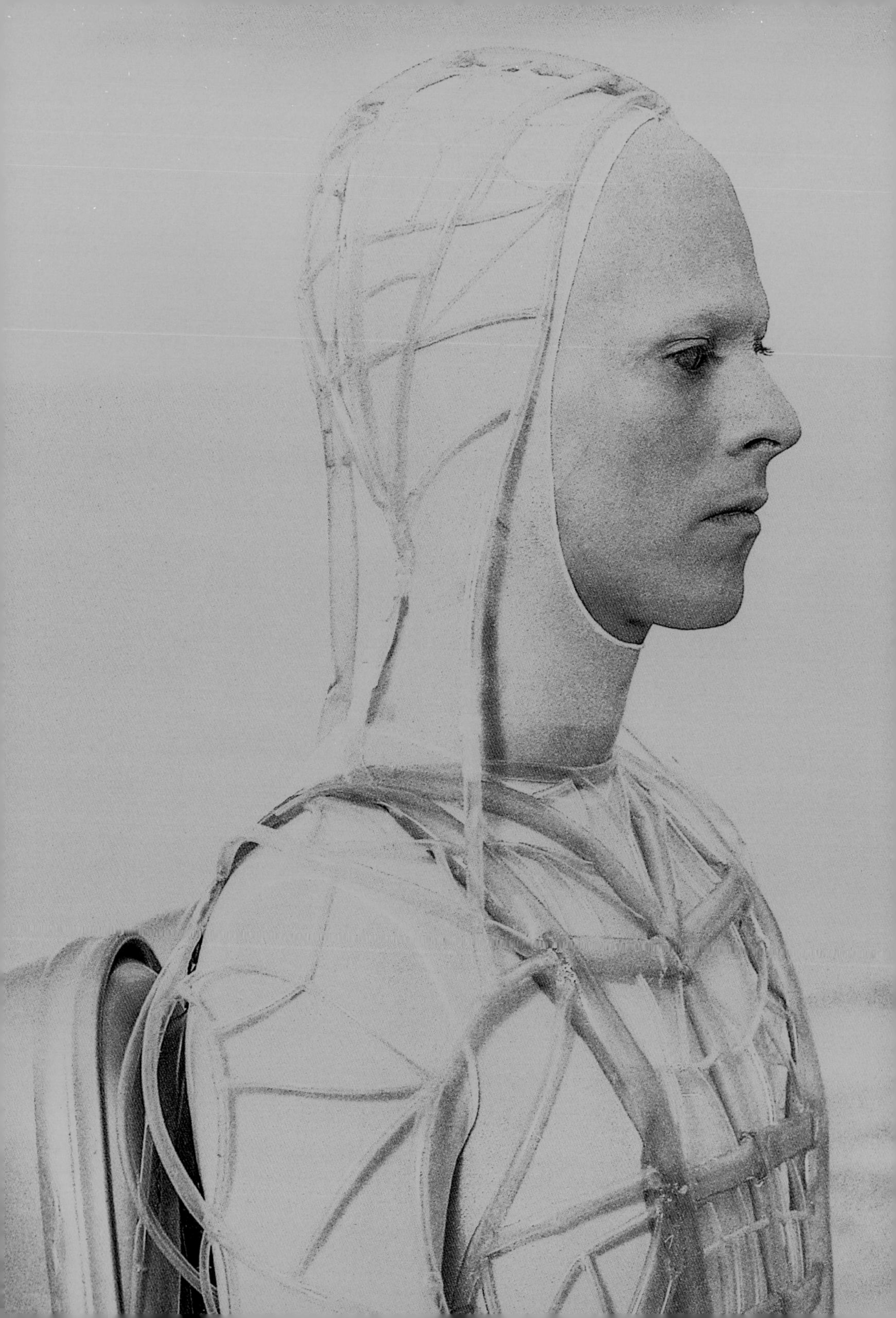

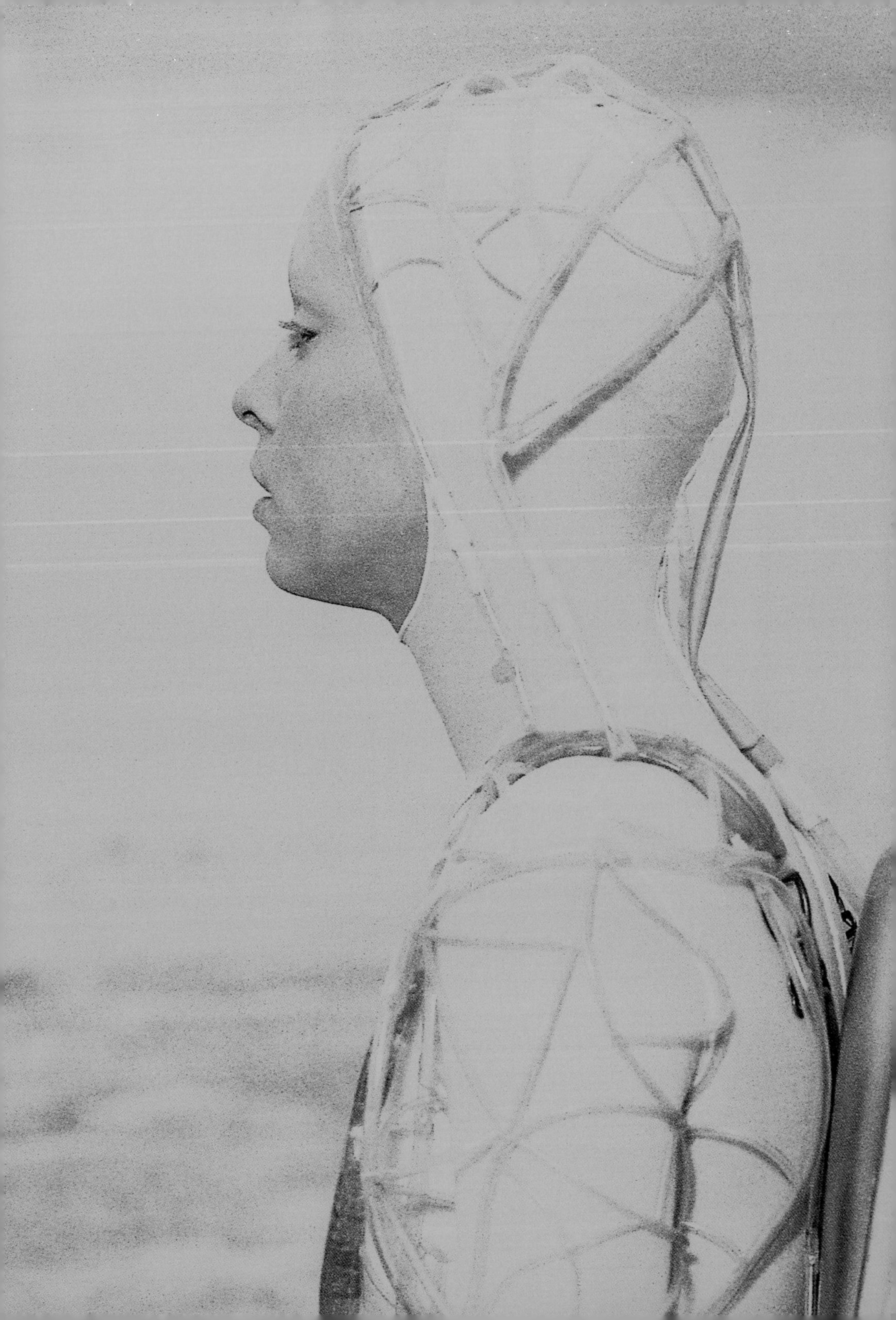

Newton reveals himself to be an alien, and tells Bryce: "I'm not a scientist. But I know all things begin and end in eternity."

WHERE HE
COMES FROM
IS AS
MYSTERIOUS
AS WHERE
HE'S GOING

Mary-Lou refuses the money offered by Farnsworth—she only wants Tommy.

NO SMOKING
SUPREME

UNLEADED

**Farnsworth and Trevor are killed as the hostile takeover of World Enterprises is put into effect. Henry: "The makeup took a couple of hours. The main problem was that I had to get up early, so I couldn't even think about going out drinking with the English crew the night before."**

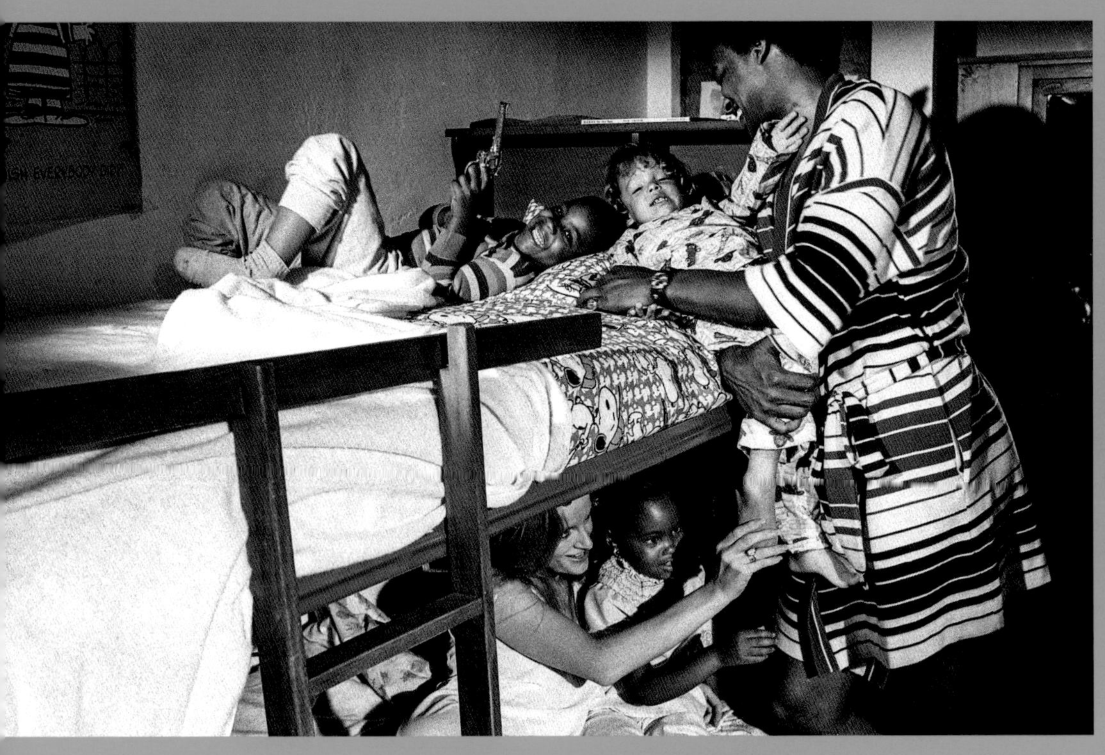

Although the dysfunctional relationship of Newton and Mary-Lou is at the heart of the film, Roeg and Mayersberg present two other couples in contrast. Oliver Farnsworth is in a homosexual partnership with Trevor, and Peters (a black former general) is married to a Caucasian woman with children. All three couples love each other, but the tragedy of the film is that Newton and Mary-Lou cannot be together.

Newton is held captive in a labyrinth of connected rooms. Bowie: "The film, I suppose, for me, is sort of allegorical on a very private scale, but it won't be to the public. They'll see more a sort of Howard Hughes figure because it's certainly an exaggeration. But it's very much the [story] of someone with a purist idea in the beginning and the whole concept becoming corrupt as it is carried out. It's a very, very sad film."

**Peters, and by implication the government, has taken over World Enterprises.**

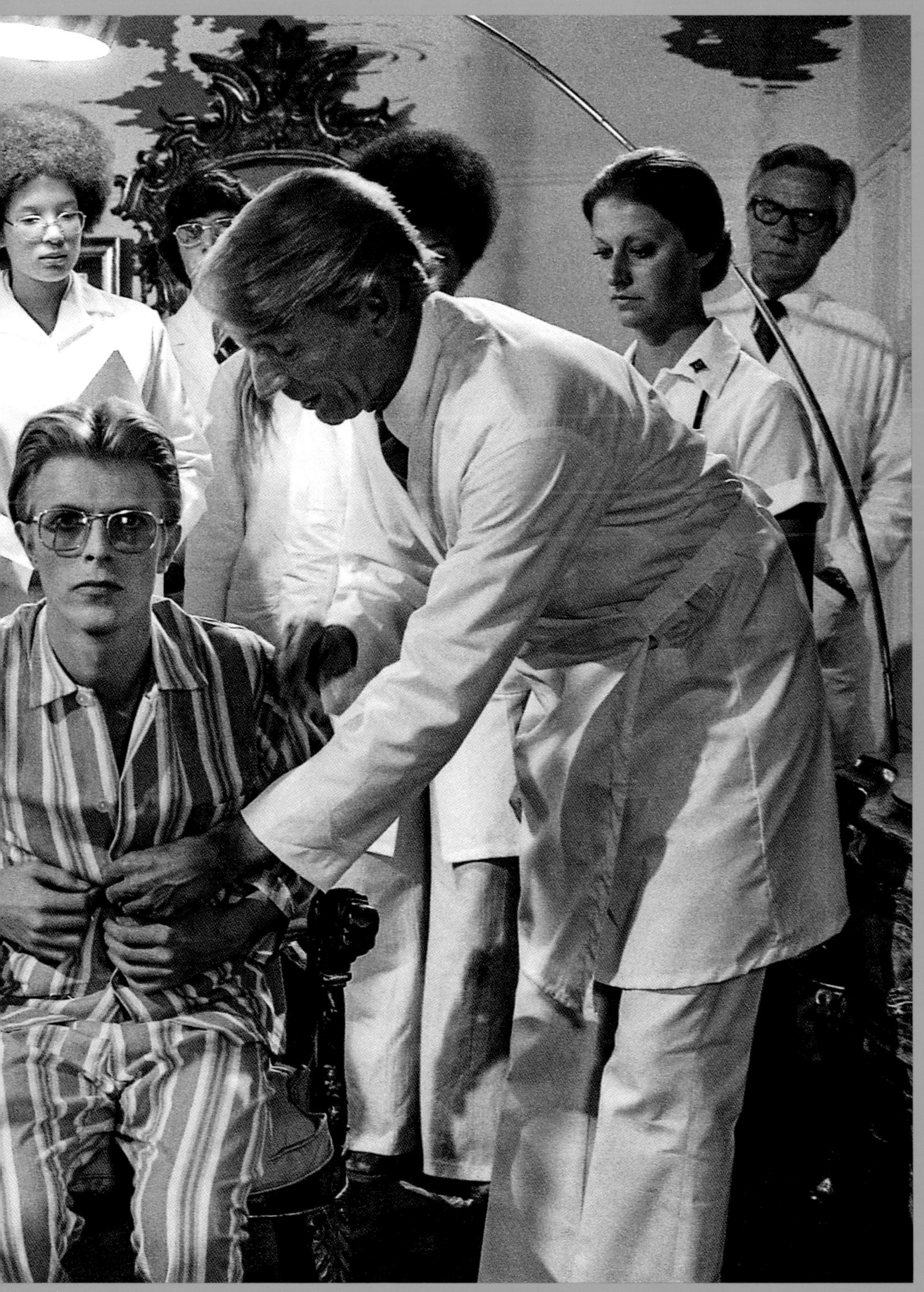

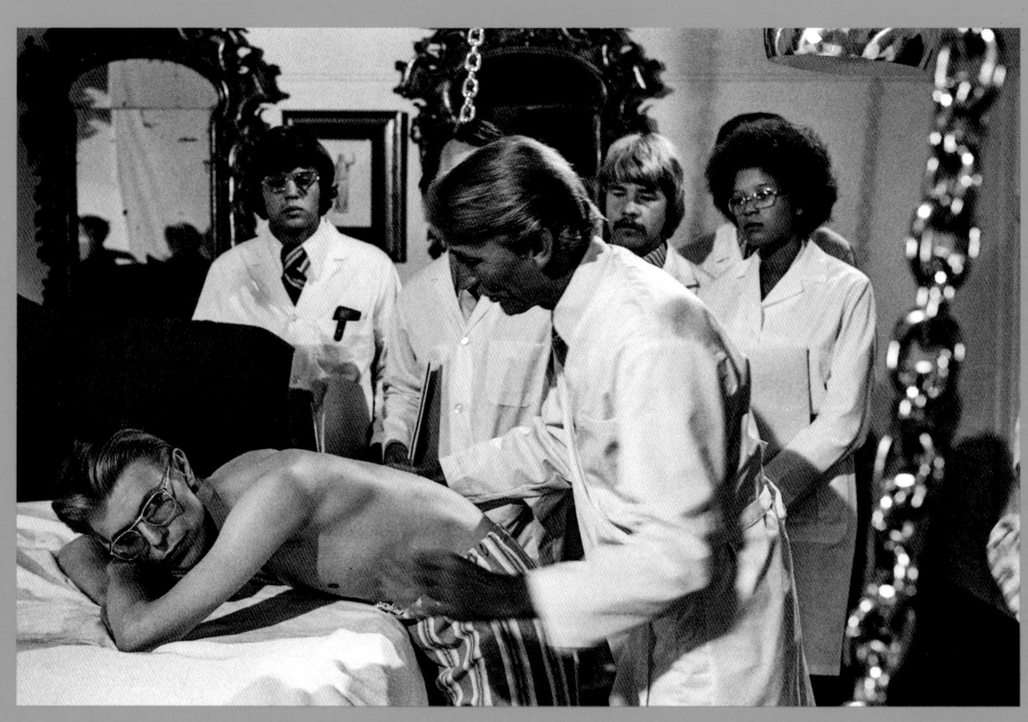

Newton is made the subject of examinations and experiments. Bowie: "For me, [Newton] wasn't Godlike at all. For me it was best exemplified by the painting—Brueghel's *Landscape with the Fall of Icarus*—that he was very much a fallible entity. I won't say God or human, because he is just a being. And his endeavors are destroyed by the beings around him."

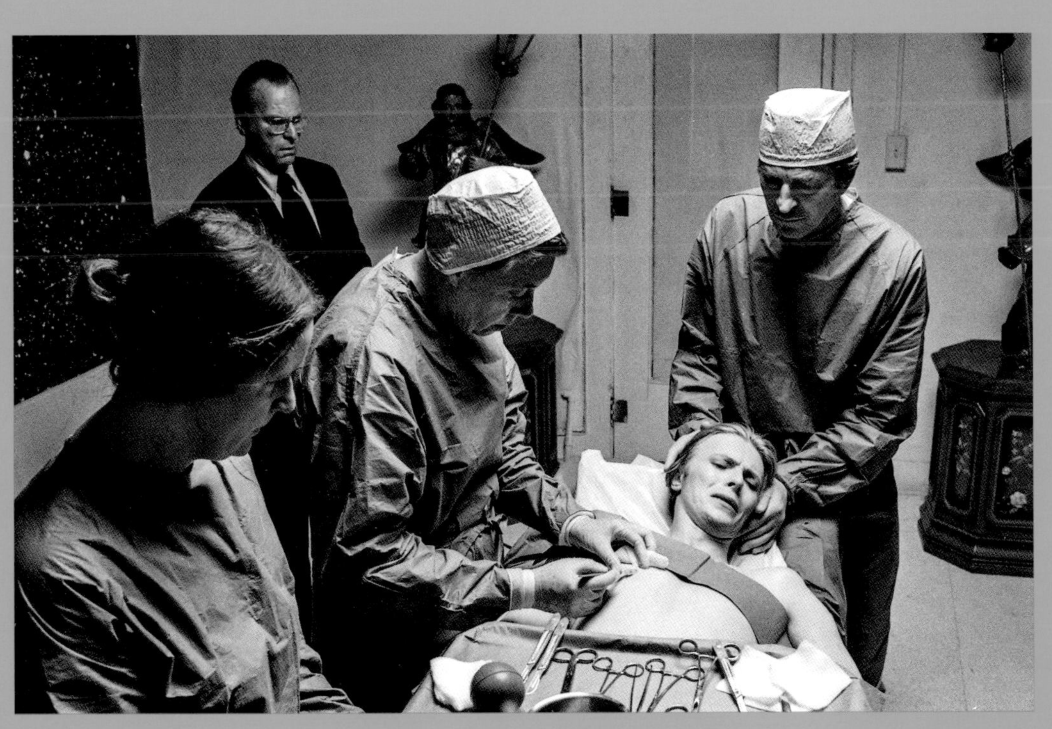

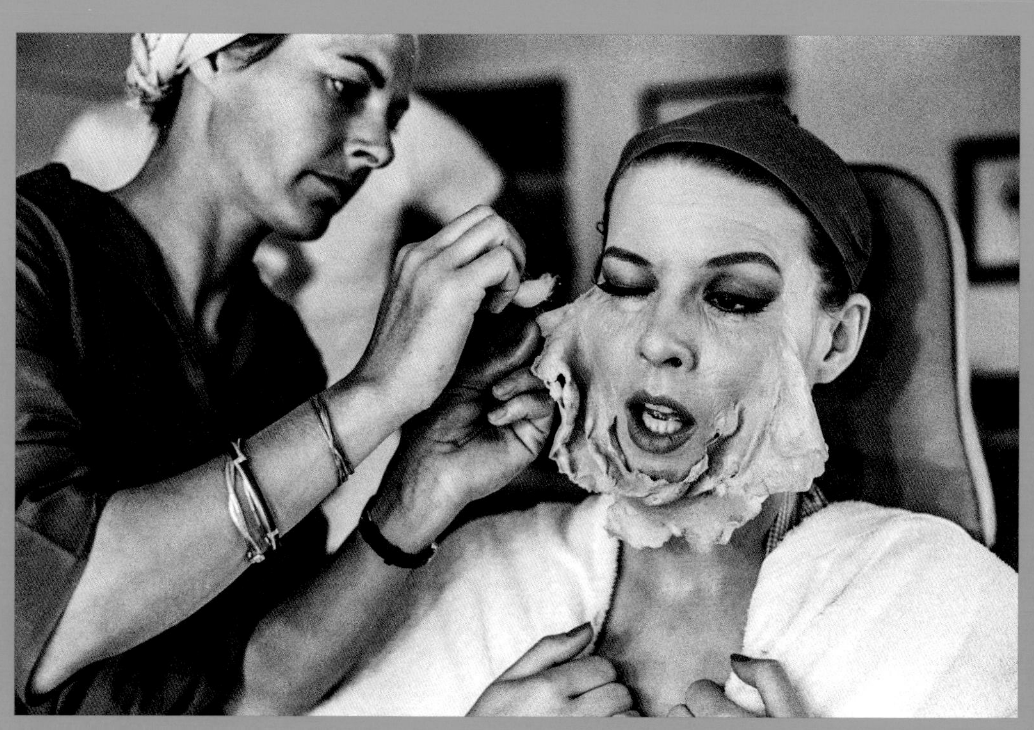

Bowie sometimes had his son, Duncan Jones, on set with him.

JACK DANIEL'S

Roeg: "It's a love story. Love stories, or stories that have a sense of love in them, are the only kind of movie I want to make. Love of individual people for each other. But it's gone by so quickly, a mistake is made, and unless it's corrected instantly, it can't be picked up again. The moment is gone."

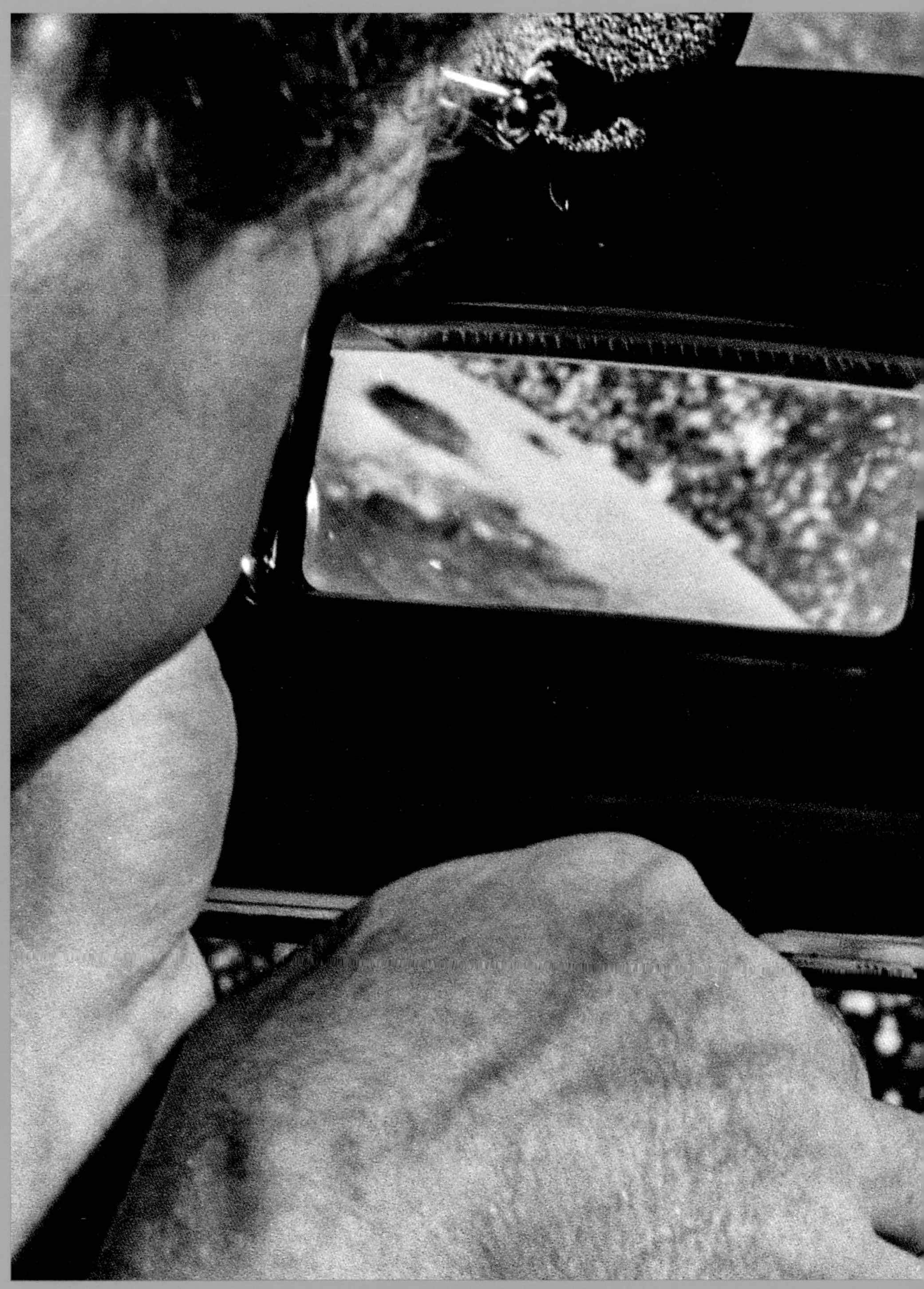

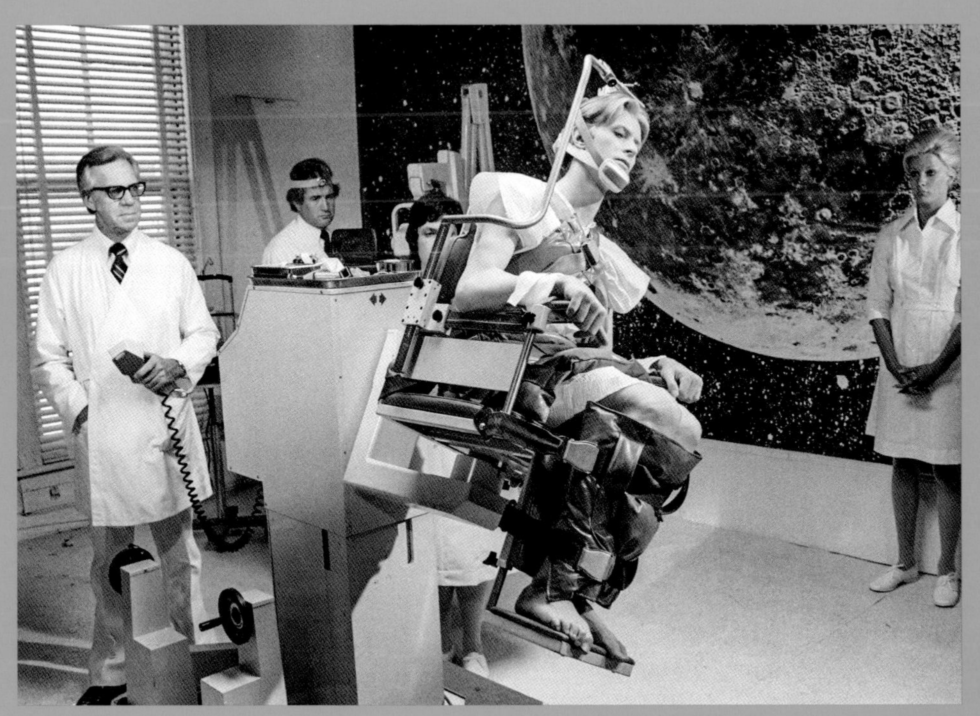

I WANT
TO GO HOME

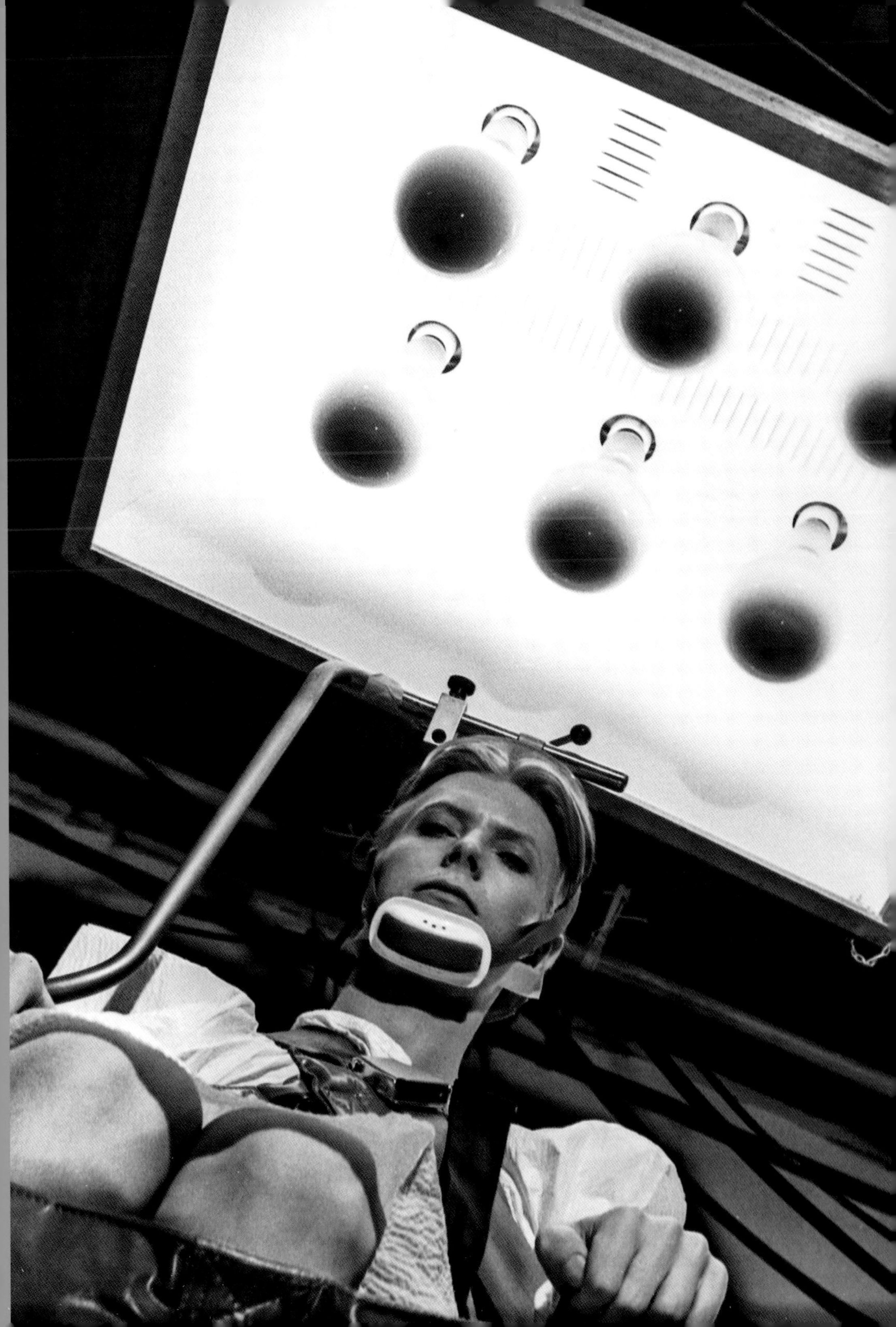

Newton sees that his family is dead, but he still lives in hope. Bowie: "I think that its basic concept of the destructive forces that we exert on ourselves and each other, the humiliation and violence and revengefulness that we bring to our relationships, is probably more understood now than it ever was then. I think [the film] pinpoints it far ahead of its time. I think it gains strength and passion through the years."

Tanqueray
Gin

Bryce buys a copy of an album by The Visitor.

WE WOULD
PROBABLY
HAVE TREATED
YOU THE SAME,
IF YOU'D
COME OVER
TO OUR PLACE

AN WHO FELL TO EARTH"
GARRETT & PTNRS
DAY / EXT
IC ROEG
8-21-75
TONY RICHMOND
802
1

# THE FALL

ESSAY BY

PAUL DUNCAN

KEATON

**A BLACK LIMOUSINE** slices its way across a bleak desert landscape. On the back seat a thin, white, fragile-looking David Bowie—a shock of orange/blond hair peeking out from under his fedora—is drinking from a milk carton as he talks about his *Diamond Dogs* tour. Bowie had been crisscrossing North America since June 1974, promoting his *Diamond Dogs* album and performing tracks like "Space Oddity," "Rebel Rebel," and "Changes." After a break in August, during which he recorded some soul songs for his next album, *Young Americans*, Bowie resumed touring until December, traveling between venues in his black limousine because he refused to fly. Asked about his tour of America, and the new music he was creating, Bowie looks into the carton: "There's a fly floating around in my milk and it's a foreign body. That's kind of how I felt. I'm a foreign body here, and I couldn't help but soak it up. It has just supplied a need in me. It has become a mythland." He continues: "There is an underlying unease [in America]. They've developed a superficial calmness to underplay the fact that there's a lot of pressure here." Bowie also feels an underlying unease in his own work. He had created Major Tom in "Space Oddity," Ziggy Stardust, and Aladdin Sane: "They are all facets of me; I got lost at one point. I couldn't decide whether I was writing characters, or the characters were writing me, or whether we were all one and the same."

Film director Nicolas Roeg saw Alan Yentob's fly-on-the-wall documentary *Cracked Actor* (broadcast by the BBC in the UK on January 26, 1975). Roeg had been working with screenwriter Paul Mayersberg on an adaption of Walter Tevis's 1963 novel *The Man Who Fell to Earth*, which is about a tall, thin, white-haired, hollow-boned alien who travels to Earth, names himself

Thomas Jerome Newton, patents many new technological advances through lawyer Oliver Farnsworth, accumulates wealth, forms a corporation, World Enterprises, and builds a spaceship for some unspecified purpose, yet remains a hermit, unknown and apart from all but a few people. Roeg had considered casting author Michael Crichton (*The Andromeda Strain*, *Westworld*, and later *Jurassic Park*) as Newton because he was 6 feet 9 inches tall, but after seeing Bowie in *Cracked Actor*, he said, "I couldn't think of anybody else for the role. I didn't know David but I'd seen his work and it became a sort of fixation because there seemed to be parallels in the attitudes and thoughts of the work that David was doing at the time."

Roeg immediately sent the script to Bowie in New York, and in February flew to New York to meet with him. "I heard that David would like to see me. He was recording and he should be finished at around 9:30 p.m. I arrived and chatted away to strangers, who were coming and going. I got a call saying that it looks like 11. By about 3 a.m. I thought that this was not going to happen. I'd already had a few martinis, so I thought that if I stay to 3, I might as well stay until 3:30. He arrived at about 5, and we spoke for about five minutes. He said, 'Don't worry. I'm going to do it. Let me know when you want me and I'll be there.' Then he showed me to the door."

Bowie. "I had known only Nic's involvement with Mick Jagger in *Performance* [1970], so I went through his previous films and I was very impressed, overwhelmed, in fact, by the work. *Walkabout* [1971] in particular really struck home. It was a wonderful film.

"I was out and when I remembered the appointment I was already an hour late, so I thought, 'Oh, no, I missed him, he won't be there now,' and just forgot about it. When I finally got home, there was

Nic waiting for me, sitting in my kitchen very patiently. Eight hours late and the man waited for me! That's persistence, isn't it?

"What I didn't tell Nic was that I wanted to kill the conversation as quickly as possible, because I didn't want Nic to suss [figure out] that I hadn't read the script. He was throwing bits of the film at me and I was saying, 'Yes. Yes. Quite. Absolutely. I can see that.' So I bluffed my way through the talk."

So why did Bowie agree to make the film? "It was a combination of having seen *Walkabout* and actually meeting Nic in person that had convinced me that this is something that I should definitely get involved with. It was probably the best decision based on absolutely nothing, other than a man's previous work, that I have ever made."

## SCRIPT

Walter Tevis's first novel, *The Hustler* (1959), became a best seller after the 1961 film adaptation, directed by Robert Rossen and starring Paul Newman, was nominated for nine Academy Awards and won two. It is the story of pool hustler "Fast Eddie" Felson, who has the skill to beat everybody. Everybody but himself.

"*The Hustler* on the surface doesn't seem to have much to do with *The Man Who Fell to Earth*," explained Mayersberg, "but in my view it's very close. American society loves a winner. It will not tolerate a loser, someone who does not achieve his aim. There's a line in *The Hustler* where Eddie hears deep inside him a voice saying, 'You don't have to be a winner.' Tevis's view was that being the best was more important than winning. There is a strong element of that in *The Man Who Fell to Earth*. Here we have a guy who is far superior to the people around him intellectually, scientifically, and so forth, yet nonetheless he loses. I think that Tevis's point is that if you have exceptional talents the world will get you.

"The other aspect from *The Hustler* is the idea of drunkenness. [Sarah Packard] is an intellectual alcoholic, writing a book. Into her life comes [Felson], an uneducated bum, but he's a genius at pool. In *The Man Who Fell to Earth*, we have a genius, Thomas Jerome Newton, who comes into the life of a completely uneducated alcoholic girl [Betty Jo] who doesn't understand what he is talking about. He comes to Earth because his planet is dry. The first thing he does is find water. He never goes anywhere where there isn't water. Newton is already a drinker before he lands. So when he meets this woman and she offers gin, water is fine for him. Everybody drinks—without water there would be no life on the planet—it's the essence of life."

*The Man Who Fell to Earth* had been optioned for film several times since its publication in 1963. Mayersberg: "It had been optioned for a TV series, much like *The Fugitive*, where each week they had to catch this alien and he got away each time. The option lapsed because nobody could lick it. It is difficult to do because there is not the budget to do everything that is in the book, and he is not the hero, he doesn't have a ray gun in his hand, and so forth

"Nic sent me *The Man Who Fell to Earth* in 1974, and what struck me was that this was not a conventional science-fiction novel. It was not, although it vaguely resembled, Robert Heinlein's *Stranger in a Strange Land* [1961]. There was no science-fiction machinery or hardware. The writer was using a science-fiction premise—the alien visiting Earth—as a pretext for a look at the United States at that time. So we took that

notion and presented the United States, largely visually, from an alien's point of view. Although he stays for many years, he finds it difficult to understand how everything works. We were less concerned about where he came from, or even why he was here, than the way someone from another planet would view ours."

Roeg: "It wasn't as though I read the book and thought, 'We can tell this story.' It seemed to me a great wheel for touching on attitudes that prevailed at the time towards so many aspects of life. Although the plot is essential, for me the plot is a shell that is inhabited by the characters. The plots of all our lives are interesting. But how we inhabit them is more interesting."

In their adaptation Mayersberg and Roeg systematically stripped back the novel to its shell and rebuilt it from the ground up. Set in 1985, 1988, and 1990, the novel follows Newton's race against time to build his spaceship.

Roeg: "We don't realize how tightly bound to time we are in our lives. Writing the script with Paul, it was surprising how often mentioning time came up, and I eliminated all that. There is never ever mention of the amount of time that has gone by in the film. I wanted to get away from the normal sense of the passage of time by dissolving and cutting from one location to another, or one person to another, or the same person in a similar or different location. Something may have happened between the cuts, but we do not know what. Time flies but it takes a long time to live. Time doesn't go by in an even way and I wanted to get a sense of that—that time wasn't particularly delineated. They age at different speeds." Over the course of the film Newton does not seem to age, although the other characters do.

As the novel progresses, Dr. Nathan Bryce, a chemistry professor, becomes a kind of detective. He sets out to find out about World Enterprises and its mystery owner, obtains a job as a top chemist on the spaceship project, and surreptitiously extracts information from Betty Jo and Newton to confirm his suspicion that Newton is an alien. Mayersberg: "It has elements of almost every genre, even the Western, partly because of the way one aspect of the story leads into another (mystery-detection-science fiction) and partly because the film is set in and about America. And America is the home of all the genres."

Several times Tevis's novel refers to *Landscape with the Fall of Icarus*, now known to be a good early copy of Pieter Bruegel's painting, as well as W. H. Auden's poem about it. Mayersberg: "What is brilliant in the painting is that no one notices the fall of Icarus, which is what Auden observed and is the basis of the poem." The painting and the poem are both shown in the film, and with enough time for the audience to read the poem. "If you look in the lower right-hand corner, there is a little figure that has splashed into the water." The painting implies humankind's indifference to suffering. "Now the idea that nobody saw him because they were all going about their business and had other things to think about intrigued us. So we created a mysterious figure who we see at the top of the coal slag heap, who is just watching. Newton says later that nobody saw him arrive, but someone did. The watcher doesn't appear again until the very end, when Newton is incarcerated. The man, incidentally, has a beard now, and he's human, because although Newton has not grown old, this curious figure has grown older like everybody else. Who is this man? He is the watcher and, in my view, the author of the piece, and he has been watching Newton all along."

The novel was set in a future where African states threaten to use nuclear weapons on each other as a deterrent. This growing threat of a nuclear holocaust—Tevis had experienced the 13 days of the Cuban missile crisis in October 1962, when the world had been on the brink of nuclear war—provides one of the reasons for Newton's presence on Earth. He is building a spaceship to send fuel to his home planet of Anthea, so that the 300 or so remaining Antheans can travel to Earth and help save it—in the past the Antheans had destroyed each other and their planet in a horrible conflict. After the CIA catches Newton, and his identity is discovered, he abandons the project, and descends into alcoholic self-oblivion.

Rather than explain Newton's plan, Mayersberg and Roeg merely gave hints in the script that Newton was planning to send water back to save his family and his unnamed planet. Their main concerns lay elsewhere.

Early in the novel, Tevis writes of Newton: "He was human; but not, properly, *a man*. Also, manlike, he was susceptible to love, to fear, to intense physical pain, and to self-pity." The novel then goes to show that the fear of discovery and of failure, combined with the intense physical pain of living on the planet (the effects of gravity, digesting food, being hurt with the slightest touch), puts so much pressure on Newton that he breaks down, finding solace for his self-pity at the bottom of a gin bottle. Missing from his life is sex (since he is not, properly, *a man*) and love.

Mayersberg: "In the book the relationship between Newton and Betty Jo was essentially platonic. That may work for him—aliens are not going to know about how sex works on Earth—but it's not going to work for her because she sure as hell knows what it is. It was something that Nic was interested in exploring because sexual relations represented danger. If you don't touch anybody, you'll be fine. The minute you touch and

CENDRILLON

go further, then danger begins. Sex is another alcohol—once you start it's very hard to stop. You get used to it and you want more of it."

Betty Jo was renamed Mary-Lou, and Candy Clark was cast in the role. Candy Clark: "Mary-Lou was a young, innocent girl who came from a very small town. She was looking for love and felt an instant affinity for Thomas Jerome Newton because he was a fragile character in need, and she was in need too because she was alone."

Roeg: "The lover's oldest question is 'What are you thinking, darling?' and then 'What are you really thinking?' Mary-Lou and Newton had been together for a while but, though she thought that he was a bit strange and odd, she had no idea where he came from. So when she says that he can tell her anything, which in the human context means 'You can tell me anything and I'll still love you,' he shows her [he is an alien and] his method of making love—by exchanging bodily fluids. Of course, she recoils."

Nathan Bryce (played by Rip Torn) was rewritten as a divorced professor fooling around with girls on campus before he begins researching World Enterprises and investigating Newton. Once Newton and Bryce meet, a friendship develops between them, although they already seem to have a psychic link. Before they meet, Newton can "hear" Bryce, and Newton even appears as an apparition while Bryce is fishing. Mayersberg: "We wanted to introduce an ESP aspect. Newton is way ahead—he knows what Bryce is thinking. Newton knows he is going to be discovered and tells Bryce, 'Don't be suspicious. Don't be afraid.' The story is what other people are doing, having to cope with the fact that Newton knows everything ahead of time."

Bryce abuses Newton's trust by secretly taking an X-ray photo of him, revealing his alien physiology. Bowie: "For me the film remains a story of betrayal that has the dressing of science fiction. The moment that Newton realizes that Bryce has taken the pictures harks back to the Bible story of Jesus knowing he is going to be betrayed by Judas. Newton knows he is going to be betrayed. It's quite obvious. But he singly doesn't do anything about it."

When Newton is on the verge of leaving after testing his spaceship, the government steps in and kidnaps him. Newton's driver hands him over, and Mary-Lou takes money to leave him. Mayersberg: "The point is—everybody betrays Newton, because when you have that ability and that power, everybody wants something from you. They want money. When the government agency comes to throw Farnsworth out of the window, it's only because he's got too much control of his company. The government wants control of the finances. What interested us was the idea that there is no division between business and politics, and I think we were quite prescient about that. It's about one company taking over another company—the fact that one company was the State is immaterial."

As for Bryce, afterwards he lives with Mary-Lou—that is his betrayal. Clark: "Mary-Lou could never really love Nathan Bryce fully because she was still focused on Newton, so they had this relationship that was always out of sync. And Thomas Jerome Newton never got over the leaving of his wife and children on the other planet. So he's stuck pining away after the unobtainable, in the same way that Mary-Lou pines after Newton. Nobody gets what they want."

Rip Torn: "The tragedy of Newton's life is that he was a failure. He was not able to save his culture. He was not able to save his family. This is the story of people who missed the boat, but they keep going."

## PRODUCTION

Roeg took the script, with Bowie attached, to various studios, and accepted an offer from Michael Deeley at British Lion. Although British Lion had a long history going back to 1927—its library included *The Third Man* (1949), *Lord of the Flies* (1963), and *The Wicker Man* (1973)—it was in a precarious financial situation. After Paramount, who had successfully distributed Roeg's previous film, *Don't Look Now* (1973) in the US, agreed to pay $1.5 million for the US rights, British Lion was able to get a loan against this contract from its bank.

Unlike the novel, the film had sequences set on Newton's home planet, for which the production needed an arid landscape. They also needed to be close to an airport so that each day's footage could be flown to Los Angeles, developed, and flown back for Roeg to review. The production settled on Albuquerque, New Mexico, as a base. For Roeg, "New Mexico has a certain mystical sense to it that I wasn't aware of," and Mayersberg notes, "there are more sightings of UFOs and aliens in New Mexico than the rest of the world put together." New Mexico is the home of the White Sands Test Facility (used by NASA and the military, and the site of the first nuclear bomb test in 1945) and of the 1947 Roswell UFO incident. Producer Michael Deeley saw other advantages: "It was out of sight of the movie unions, and [Albuquerque] being, at that time, not too prosperous a town, we were welcome to go there and spend our money. There was a new Hilton Hotel which housed the crew for $15 each a night and gave us parking for our trucks. If I had hired a crew in Hollywood the cost would have been impossibly expensive, so we decided to take a gamble. Each member of the crew went to the US Embassy in Grosvenor Square, London, and lodged an individual application for a tourist visa. We charted an Aer Lingus plane and loaded as much of the equipment as we could carry with the entire film crew already aboard, and then flew to Albuquerque. Two days later the unit started shooting. This was the first time—and will probably stand as the last time—that a full-sized British crew shot an entire feature film in America."

"This was my first time in America. I loved it then and still do," remembers still photographer David James, echoing a sentiment felt by the rest of the crew. Bowie and his friend Geoff MacCormack (who performed as Bowie's backup singer as "Warren Peace") took the train from Los Angeles to Albuquerque, and stayed at the Hilton. James: "Most of the English crew stayed in the hotel, a few rented out their own places. Nic liked to shoot at first light, so generally we got up at around 6–6:30 a.m. and would go to the set to have breakfast. We would get call sheets, and most of us had cars, so we'd drive ourselves to the locations. New Mexico in the morning was beautiful. It was a communal atmosphere and we occasionally spent breakfast comparing hangovers. Eventually Nic and the DP [Director of Photography, Anthony Richmond] would arrive and work out the scene for the day. Then the actors would turn up and go through rehearsals."

Filming on the 11-week shoot began on Monday, June 2, 1975, in Los Lunas—Roeg considered the place (it translates as "The Moons") an auspicious sign—with Newton walking into Haneyville, selling a gold ring, and drinking water collected from the Rio Grande. James: "We didn't mess about. We moved very fast on the setups."

As Newton walks into the town he goes past an abandoned fairground and a drunk begins to harangue him. Bowie: "The first thing Newton sees in connection to a human is the effect of the alcohol which is going to destroy him, or at least keep him here." Then a big gust of wind comes and lifts a fairground inflatable up in the air. Roeg: "The balloon broke free and came bouncing down towards us. I told them not to cut, to carry on."

James: "Fats Domino came to the Hilton with his band, and thanks to David, Geoff MacCormack and I got to sit at the front." A good number of Budweisers were consumed. Geoff MacCormack: "As nine-year-olds, David and I had bought 'Blueberry Hill,' so we were really looking forward to seeing the man himself perform it live. Afterwards we stumbled backstage. We knocked on the fat man's door and from inside there came a booming voice. 'Who is it?' 'David Bowie.' 'Who?' 'David Bowie, from London.' 'David *who*?'" Some girls knocked on the door and gained immediate entry. Bowie tried again. "The door opened and there, looking down on us, was the biggest black man I'd ever seen. He informed us that Mr. Domino was busy right now, then closed the door in our faces. David took no insult from this episode. On the contrary, it was all just too amusing." James: "We went into the coffee shop afterwards with some members of the band and Bowie was dancing on the tables. The women at the coffee shop were shouting at him to get off the tables or they'd call the police. 'Call them. Call them,' Bowie told them."

MacCormack: "After some time staying at the Hilton, David rented a ranch-style bungalow near Santa Fe, and his PA, Coco [Schwab], and I moved in with him. David used the bright conservatory to start painting again." Between scenes Bowie wrote new songs and stories, including his proposed autobiography, *The Return of the Thin White Duke*.

The Hotel Artesia in Artesia was a key location. Most of the hotel was unused, so the production had free rein to knock down walls and dress the rooms as they

wished. Not only was it used for Newton's arrival at the hotel, the elevator scene, and the hotel-room scenes with Mary-Lou, but it also served for the place of Newton's incarceration by the government.

James: "Nic would create a set and then put the characters into it. That was his magic. They rehearsed. They read through the dialogue, and there would be inevitable change to some of it. Next Nic would have them rehearse the scene, and he'd block out where the cameras are going to be. He was soft-spoken on set, always with his quiet British sense of humor."

Clark: "David wasn't a person who ever expressed what he was feeling, so you never knew what was going on inside him. Plus, he only spent time with his entourage. So outside of acting together, we never had dinner or spent any non-working time together. He was very removed and quiet and of course this was perfect for me, because my character never knew what was going on inside Thomas Newton."

Bowie: "It was the first thing I'd ever done. I was ignorant of the established procedure [of making movies], so I was going a lot on instinct, and my instinct was pretty dissipated. I just learned the lines for that day and did them the way I was feeling. I actually was feeling as alienated as that character was. It was a pretty natural performance...a good exhibition of somebody literally falling apart in front of you. I was totally insecure with about 10 grams [of cocaine] a day in me. I was stoned out of my mind from beginning to end."

Production designer Brian Eatwell built an exterior for Newton's Japanese-style home at the edge of Fenton Lake, 80 miles north of Albuquerque in the Jemez Mountains, and west of Los Alamos, where the Manhattan Project was based. (The interiors of the house, which had round adobe walls so that Newton would not hurt himself, were filmed in Santa Fe.) Across the lake, the park ranger's cabin was dressed as Nathan Bryce's house.

The lake was stocked with trout. James: "Rip Torn and I had a common interest in fly fishing. One evening, when we were shooting on the wooden jetty at the lake, at wrap the grips and some of the local guys lit a little campfire and set up a pot of boiling water. Rip taught us how to catch crayfish; we'd catch them, throw them into the pot, and eat them."

Bowie: "I loved Rip—he was a wonderful guy—there was something of Hemingway or Mailer about him. He had a great manly way. Every day and night was a huge adventure for Rip. We were all agape every morning, waiting to hear about his exploits. 'I'll tell you what happened last night...' he'd begin. He'd climb through barbwire fences, and be found in ditches.

"Rip came on set one day in a particularly stumpy mood. For some reason, he had it in for Nic and growled, 'If you're going to treat me like a dog then I'm going to react like a dog.' Nic looked at him and said to the cameraman, 'We won't be shooting Mr. Torn today,' and just left him there on the set, fuming."

White Sands near Alamogordo supplied the setting for the alien world, with Bowie, Clark, and two child actors playing the alien family. They wore skin-tight suits encased in a lacelike web of tubing containing precious water. The predominant facial feature of the aliens was their catlike eyes. Bowie: "In those days, contact lenses tended to be made of hard plastic and they really, really hurt the eyes badly. I was particularly dehydrated and the desert didn't help." Roeg: "When Candy went to get her contacts fitted, the contact just sucked onto her eyeball. It fitted too well. It took over an hour for the doctor to work out how to get the lens out."

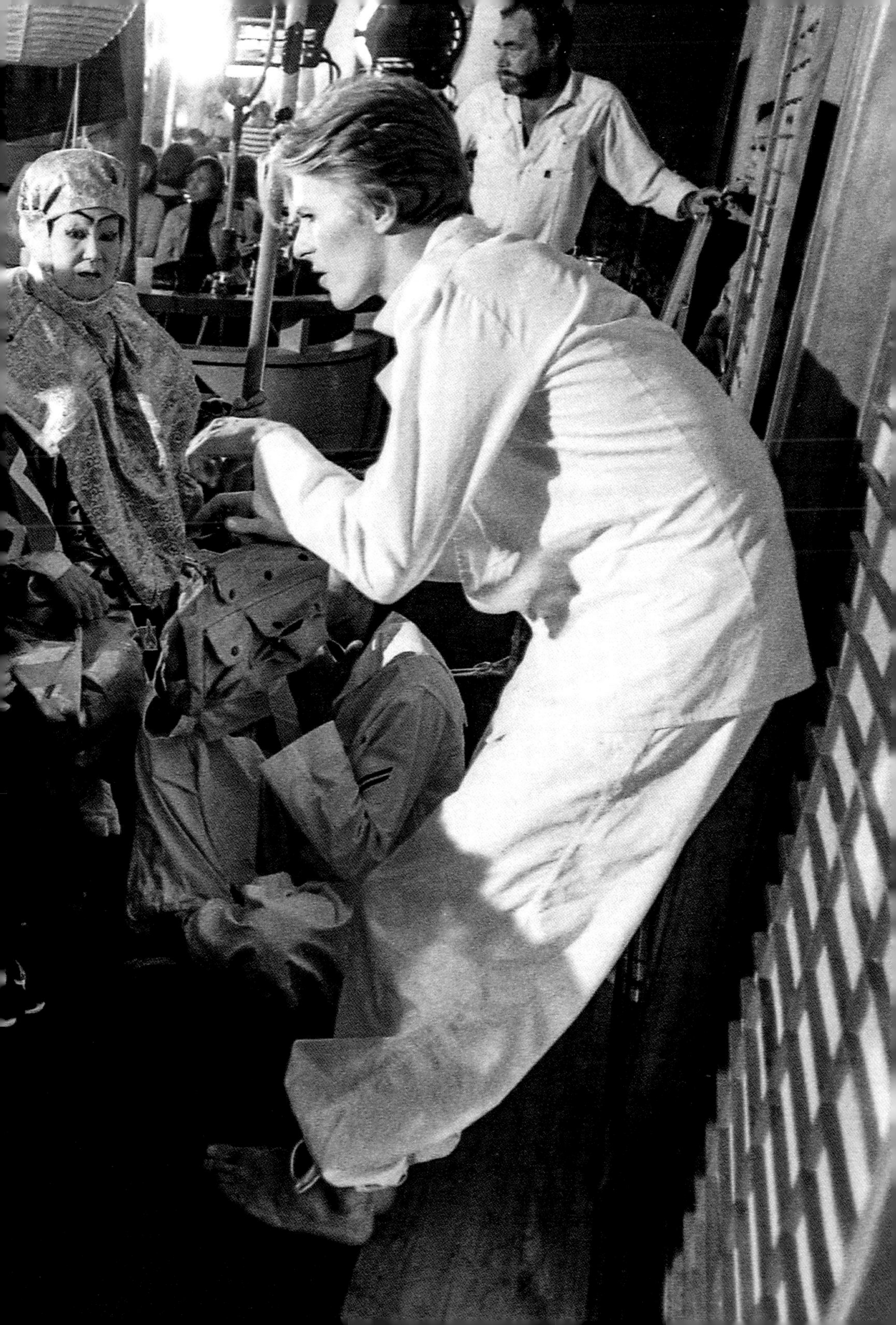

MINI MOBILE FILM VAN
PRODUCTION SYSTEMS, INC.
DRIV

There are visual and textual references to trains throughout the film, since, for Newton, it represents the last time he saw his family, when he departed on the alien train. To visualize this scene in the film, Brian Eatwell laid a monorail track on the desert floor, and built the alien train around an old tractor. The train had an organic surface and was fitted with solar sails. Bowie: "When the train turned up, it was nothing like what Nic had envisaged. He went blue in the face, then he went red, then white and he said, 'What is that?' 'It's your train, sir.' 'That's not a train, it's a fucking dog kennel!' But we lived with it." The shoot was further complicated when the tractor broke down. Unable to replace the parts, they attached ropes to the train and had horses pull it out of shot. James: "Such problems are normal on a film."

After 10 weeks of shooting in New Mexico, the production moved to Los Angeles for the last few days. James: "We had to do it secretly because of the LA unions and work permits." Bowie rented a house in Bel-Air and began recording at Cherokee Studios on non-filming days.

At Tower Records on the Sunset Strip, an elderly Bryce buys a record by The Visitor (aka Newton). Copies of Bowie's *Young Americans* album can be seen on sale in the background. The Kabuki performance, which Newton walks out of because he is upset by the violence, was shot in a Japanese restaurant, also on Sunset. The final meeting between Bryce and Newton was filmed at Butterfield's restaurant on Sunset Boulevard. Roeg: "It's such a financially driven business that it encourages the belief that everything is linear. In the first scene, Newton passes a children's fairground. Just as we were passing, an old tramp in one of the rides sat up and belched. There's no way we could have planned that. The first human noise in the film is a belch and so is the last one, where Bowie burps at his table. I like the idea of chance. You have to see the different things around you while you're filming. What makes God laugh is people who make plans."

## POSTPRODUCTION

Roeg returned to the UK to edit the movie with Graeme Clifford. Deeley: "The original plan was to have David Bowie provide the music for the film." Bowie: "I spent two or three months putting bits and pieces of material together." However, the compositions he delivered were rejected by Roeg. Paul Buckmaster, a cellist who had arranged Bowie's "Space Oddity," worked on the sessions with Bowie and suggests why the music wasn't used: "Firstly it was just not up to the standard of composing and performance needed for a good movie; secondly, I don't think it fitted well to the picture; and lastly, it wasn't really what Nic Roeg was looking for." Deeley: "Nic's editor, Graeme Clifford, then wanted to use some Pink Floyd tracks, but they were unobtainable and would in any case have been too expensive. In the end, John Phillips, once of The Mamas and the Papas, put together a combination of some new tracks and some existing cuts." In fact, Phillips had heard Bowie's score, and later described it as "haunting and beautiful, with chimes, Japanese bells, and what sounded like electronic winds and waves." This description could also fit the six tracks by Japanese progressive-rock composer Stomu Yamashta that were used at key moments in the film. As for Bowie's demo tracks, he said, "Some of it went onto *Station to Station*, but another chunk of it became the album *Low*, which I did with Brian Eno in Berlin a few years later."

Deeley: "While the music was being painstakingly added, I took a rough cut to New York to show to the newly appointed chairman of Paramount Pictures, Barry Diller. The viewing by Paramount would trigger their first payment to us under British Lion's contract. For a few minutes after the lights came up at the end of the screening, Diller said nothing. Finally, he said, 'This is not the movie Paramount bought. The picture we bought is linear, and this isn't,' and he now indicated his disinclination to honor the deal his company had struck prior to his tenure. This was a potential disaster for British Lion. No other major US distributor would want to pick up *The Man Who Fell to Earth* because it was now soiled goods, blighted by Paramount's rejection. Hollywood is highly superstitious."

Eventually, Don Rugoff of Cinema V paid an advance of $850,000 for the US release.

## RELEASE

*The Man Who Fell to Earth* premiered at the Leicester Square Theatre, London, on March 18, 1976. It received mixed reviews. Roeg: "One critic complained about the line 'All things begin and end in eternity.' I told him, 'You realize that's [William] Blake?'" Upon first viewing, it was difficult to see the various plot threads, visual motifs, and themes that glued the film together because of its elliptical editing scheme. Roeg had changed the film grammar, "by taking away the crutch of time, which the audience usually holds onto. I think the film is rather like a lifetime that goes in fits and starts. At the end of people's lives, it is difficult to find what the actual story is." Roeg wanted the audience to "read the screen," and let the movie "work on them."

Cinema V released the film in the US on May 28, but they exercised their right to cut the film—it was reduced by 20 minutes—leaving Roeg "totally distressed and upset." The reviews were equally mixed.

Over the past 40 years the film has grown in stature, not least because the film grammar that Roeg pioneered in *The Man Who Fell to Earth* has been assimilated by subsequent filmmakers, and audiences have learned to "read the screen." Bowie: "I had already been tantalized by the idea of fragmentation because I was quite a fan of William S. Burroughs's cut-ups. Nic realized that two things colliding can present a third piece of information that none of us were aware of, and it would delight him when he saw these coincidences make sense, this order coming out of chaos. The order in chaos is now a substantial theory in science. I took away that element and invested it in a lot of my subsequent work, and I guess it reached its zenith with my work with Brian Eno. My work was certainly informed by the coincidence and fragmentation process of working on this film with Nic."

At the end of the movie, Bryce tracks down Newton through a record of "poetry and music you have never heard before" by The Visitor. "Did you like it?" Newton asks. "Not much," Bryce replies. "Well," Newton says, "I didn't make it for you, anyway." Newton vainly hopes that it will be played on the radio and someday reach the family he left behind. But Roeg understands the real tragedy of the situation, one that is perhaps the source of Newton's pain: "He's no longer a visitor. He's one of us."

AIRLIFT

# *DER STURZ*

von Paul Duncan

Eine schwarze Limousine gleitet durch eine öde Wüstenlandschaft. Im Fond sitzt ein schlanker, fahler, zerbrechlich wirkender David Bowie. Ein orangeblonder Haarschopf lugt unter seinem Fedorahut hervor, und während er aus einer Milchtüte trinkt, redet er über seine *Diamond Dogs*-Tour. Seit Juli 1974 war Bowie kreuz und quer durch Nordamerika gereist, hatte die Werbetrommel für sein Album *Diamond Dogs* gerührt und trat mit Songs wie *Space Oddity*, *Rebel Rebel* und *Changes* auf. Nach einer Pause im August, in der er ein paar Soulnummern für sein nächstes Album – *Young Americans* – eingespielt hatte, setzte Bowie bis Dezember seine Tour fort und ließ sich in seiner schwarzen Limousine von Auftritt zu Auftritt chauffieren, weil er sich weigerte zu fliegen. Als er nach seiner Amerikatournee und nach der neuen Musik, die er schrieb, gefragt wird, schaut er in seine Milchtüte: „Da schwimmt eine Fliege in meiner Milch, und sie ist ein Fremdkörper. In etwa so habe ich mich gefühlt. Ich bin hier ein Fremdkörper,

und ich musste es einfach in mich aufsaugen. Es stillte ein inneres Bedürfnis in mir. Es wurde zu einem Märchenland." Er fährt fort: „Man spürt hier überall eine innere Unruhe. Nach außen hin strahlen [die Amerikaner] eine gewisse Ruhe aus, um die Tatsache zu überspielen, dass hier eine Menge Druck ausgeübt wird." Bowie spürt diese Unruhe auch in seiner Arbeit. Für *Space Oddity* hatte er Major Tom geschaffen, Ziggy Stardust und Aladdin Sane: „Sie alle sind ein Teil von mir. Einmal verlor ich die Orientierung. Ich konnte mich nicht mehr entscheiden, ob ich die Figuren schrieb oder die Figuren mich oder ob wir nicht alle ein und dieselbe Person waren."

Der Regisseur Nicolas Roeg sah sich Alan Yentobs Dokumentation *Cracked Actor* (in Großbritannien und Nordirland am 26. Januar 1975 von der BBC ausgestrahlt) an, als er gerade mit Drehbuchautor Paul Mayersberg an einer Verfilmung von Walter Tevis' Roman *Der Mann, der vom Himmel fiel* (1963) arbeitete. Das Buch handelt von einem großen, schlanken, weißhaarigen, hohlknochigen Außerirdischen, der zur Erde reist, sich Thomas Jerome Newton nennt, durch den Anwalt Oliver Farnsworth mehrere technische Innovationen patentieren lässt, reich wird, eine Firma namens World Enterprises gründet und zu irgendeinem unbestimmten Zweck ein Raumschiff baut, dabei aber ein Eigenbrötler bleibt, der sich von der Welt abschottet und zu nur wenigen Menschen Kontakt pflegt. Ursprünglich hatte Roeg die Rolle mit dem Schriftsteller Michael Crichton (*Andromeda*, *Westworld* und später *Jurassic Park*) besetzen wollen, weil dieser 2,06 Meter groß war, aber nachdem er Bowie in *Cracked Actor* gesehen hatte, meinte er: „Ich konnte mir niemand anderen in der Rolle vorstellen. Ich kannte David nicht, aber ich kannte seine Arbeit, und es wurde zu einer Art fixer Idee, weil es Parallelen

zu geben schien zwischen den Standpunkten und Gedanken des Werks und dem, was David zu dieser Zeit machte."

Umgehend schickte Roeg das Drehbuch nach New York, wo sich Bowie gerade aufhielt, und flog im Februar selbst dorthin, um sich mit ihm zu treffen. „Ich hatte gehört, dass David mich sehen wollte. Er machte gerade Aufnahmen und sollte gegen 21:30 Uhr fertig sein. Ich kam und unterhielt mich mit Fremden, die dort ein und aus gingen. Ich erhielt einen Anruf, dass es elf werden könnte. Gegen drei Uhr dachte ich, jetzt sei das Treffen wohl gestorben. Ich hatte schon ein paar Martinis intus, und da dachte ich mir, wenn ich schon mal bis drei geblieben war, dann konnte ich auch bis halb vier warten. Er kam gegen fünf, und wir unterhielten uns etwa fünf Minuten lang. Er sagte: ‚Machen Sie sich keine Sorgen. Ich werd's machen. Lassen Sie mich wissen, wann Sie mich brauchen, und ich werde da sein.' Dann schickte er mich raus."

Bowie: „Ich kannte Nics Arbeit nur aus *Performance* [1970] mit Mick Jagger, also schaute ich mir seine früheren Filme an, und ich war von seiner Arbeit tief beeindruckt, sogar überwältigt. Insbesondere *Walkabout* [1971] traf voll ins Schwarze. Es war ein wunderbarer Film.

Ich war aus, und als ich mich an die Verabredung erinnerte, war es schon eine Stunde zu spät, also dachte ich: ‚Oh nein, ich habe ihn verpasst. Er wird jetzt nicht mehr da sein', und vergaß ihn einfach. Als ich schließlich nach Hause kam, saß Nic in meiner Küche und wartete mit einer Engelsgeduld auf mich. Ich kam acht Stunden zu spät, und der Mensch hatte auf mich gewartet! Wenn das kein Durchhaltevermögen ist!

Was ich Nic nicht verriet, war, dass ich das Gespräch möglichst rasch abwürgen wollte, weil ich nicht wollte, dass er spitzkriegte, dass ich das Drehbuch gar nicht

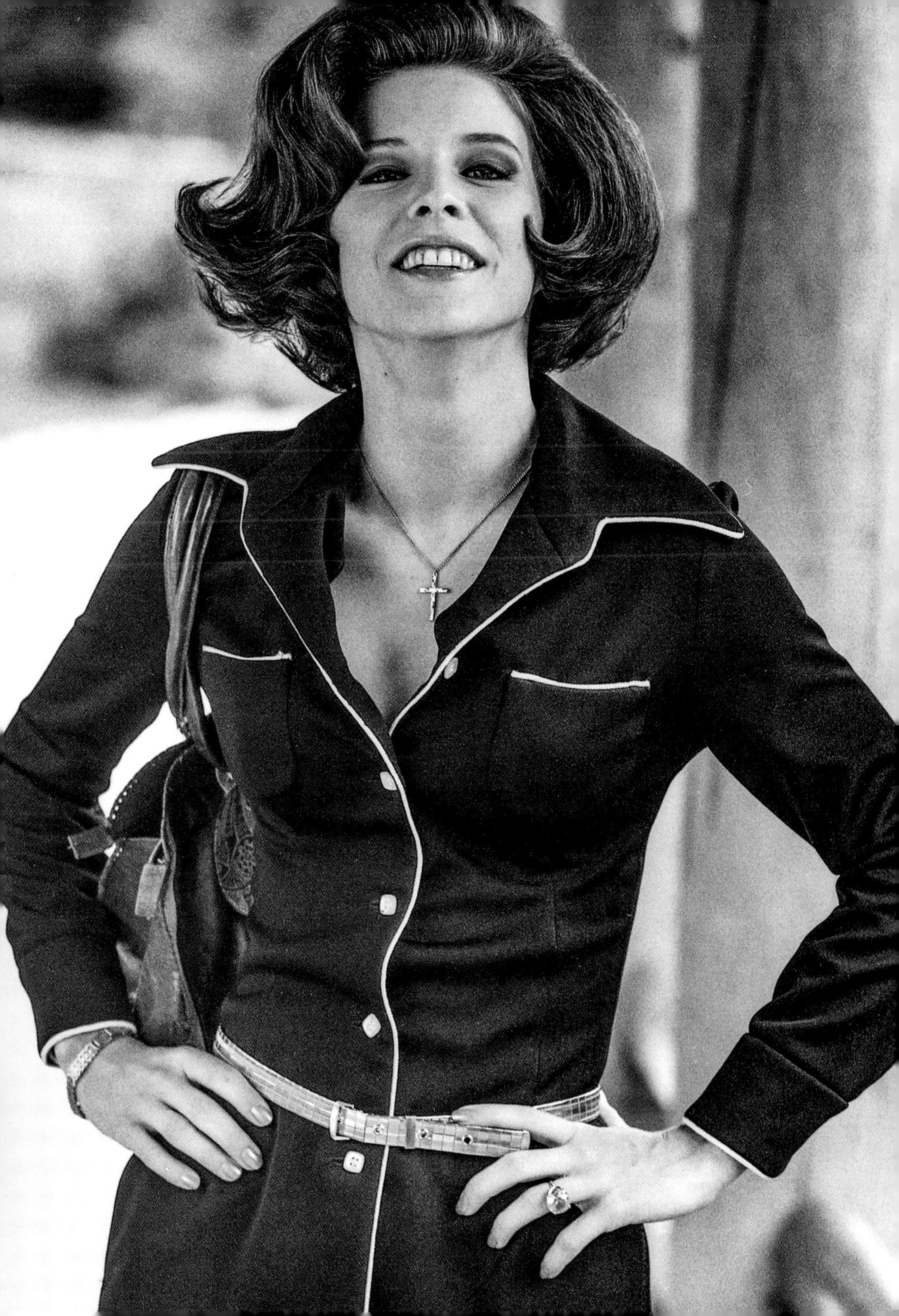

gelesen hatte. Er warf mir Brocken aus dem Film an den Kopf, und ich sagte nur: ‚Ja. Ja. Genau. Absolut. Ich seh's vor mir.' So hangelte ich mich durch das Gespräch."

Weshalb aber ließ er sich dann auf den Film ein? „Einerseits, weil ich *Walkabout* gesehen hatte, andererseits, weil ich Nic persönlich getroffen hatte. Beides überzeugte mich, dass dies etwas war, an dem ich unbedingt beteiligt sein sollte. Es war vermutlich die beste Entscheidung meines Lebens, die auf absolut nichts anderem gründete als der vorherigen Arbeit einer Person."

## DREHBUCH

Walter Tevis' erster Roman *The Hustler* (1959) wurde nach der gleichnamigen Verfilmung von 1961 (deutscher Verleihtitel: *Haie der Großstadt*) unter der Regie von Robert Rossen und mit Paul Newman in der Hauptrolle zum Bestseller. Der Film wurde für neun Oscars nominiert und gewann zwei. Es ist die Geschichte eines Poolbillardabzockers namens „Fast Eddie" Felson, der mit allem und jedem fertigwerden konnte – außer mit sich selbst.

„Oberflächlich betrachtet, schien *Haie der Großstadt* nicht viel mit *Der Mann, der vom Himmel fiel* gemein zu haben", erklärte Mayersberg, „doch meiner Meinung nach sind sie sich sehr ähnlich. Die amerikanische Gesellschaft liebt Sieger. Sie duldet keine Verlierer – Leute, die ihr Ziel nicht erreichen. Es gibt eine Stelle im Film, an der Eddie tief in seinem Inneren eine Stimme sagen hört: ‚Du musst kein Sieger sein.' Tevis war der Ansicht, dass es wichtiger sei, der Beste zu sein, als zu gewinnen. Das spielt auch eine zentrale Rolle in *Der Mann, der vom Himmel fiel*. Da ist dieser

Typ, der seinem Umfeld intellektuell, wissenschaftlich und so fort weit überlegen ist, aber trotzdem verliert er. Ich glaube, dass Tevis uns damit sagen will: Wenn du außergewöhnliche Begabungen hast, dann wird die Welt dich kriegen.

Der andere Aspekt von *The Hustler* ist der Umgang mit Alkohol. [Sarah Packard] ist eine intellektuelle Alkoholikerin, die ein Buch schreibt. Sie lernt [Felson] kennen, einen ungebildeten Penner, der aber ein Genie beim Pool ist. In *Der Mann, der vom Himmel fiel* haben wir ein Genie, Thomas Jerome Newton, das in das Leben eines völlig ungebildeten, alkoholabhängigen Mädchens [Betty Jo] tritt, das nicht versteht, wovon er redet. Er kommt zur Erde, weil sein Planet trocken ist. Als Erstes sucht er Wasser. Er geht niemals irgendwohin, wo es kein Wasser gibt. Newton ist bereits ein Trinker, bevor er landet. Als er also diese Frau trifft und sie ihm Gin anbietet, ist das für ihn in Ordnung. Jeder trinkt – ohne Wasser gäbe es kein Leben auf dem Planeten, es ist die Essenz des Lebens."

Seit der Veröffentlichung des Romans 1963 hatte es bereits mehrere Angebote gegeben, *Der Mann, der vom Himmel fiel* zu verfilmen. Mayersberg: „Man hatte ihn für eine Fernsehserie à la *Auf der Flucht* optioniert, in der man diesen Außerirdischen Woche für Woche jagen ließe und er immer wieder entkäme. Diese Option verfiel, weil niemand damit klarkam. Mit knappem Budget ist es schwierig, alles, was in dem Buch vorkommt, umzusetzen, und er ist nicht der Held, der mit einer Laserpistole durch die Gegend rennt und so weiter.

Nic schickte mir *Der Mann, der vom Himmel fiel* 1974. Mir fiel auf, dass es kein typischer Science-Fiction-Roman war. Es war – trotz einer gewissen Ähnlichkeit – nicht wie Robert Heinleins *Fremder in einer fremden Welt* [1961]. Es gab keine Science-Fiction-Maschinen oder -Geräte. Der Autor verwendete eine Science-

Fiction-Prämisse – der Außerirdische, der die Erde besucht – als Vorwand für eine Betrachtung der Vereinigten Staaten zur damaligen Zeit. Wir griffen diese Idee auf und präsentierten die USA, hauptsächlich visuell, aus der Sicht eines Außerirdischen. Auch wenn er viele Jahre bleibt, ist für ihn immer noch schwer zu verstehen, wie alles funktioniert. Uns interessierte weniger, woher er kommt oder weshalb er hier ist, sondern vielmehr, wie jemand von einem anderen Planeten den unseren sehen würde."

Roeg: „Es war nicht so, dass ich das Buch gelesen und gedacht hätte: ‚Diese Geschichte können wir erzählen.' Mir schien, es greife wie die Zähne eines Zahnrads die Standpunkte zu diversen Aspekten des Lebens auf, die zur damaligen Zeit vorherrschten. Wenngleich die Handlung wesentlich ist, so ist sie für mich doch nur eine Hülle, die von den Charakteren bewohnt wird. Die Rahmenhandlung unseres Lebens ist interessant. Doch wie wir sie mit Leben füllen, ist interessanter."

Für ihre Adaption reduzierten Mayersberg und Roeg den Roman systematisch auf seine Hülle und setzten ihn von Grund auf neu zusammen. Der Roman, der in den Jahren 1985, 1988 und 1990 spielt, folgt Newtons Versuch, im Wettlauf gegen die Zeit ein Raumschiff fertigzustellen.

Roeg: „Wir merken gar nicht, wie eng wir in unserem Leben an die Zeit gebunden sind. Als Paul und ich das Drehbuch schrieben, waren wir überrascht, wie oft Zeit thematisiert wurde, und ich strich das alles heraus. An keiner Stelle im Film wird erwähnt, wie viel Zeit vergangen ist. Ich wollte mich vom normalen Zeitgefühl lösen, indem ich von einem Schauplatz zum anderen überblendete oder -schnitt oder von einer Person zu einer anderen oder von der gleichen Person an einen ähnlichen oder anderen Ort. Zwischen den Schnitten mag etwas vorgefallen sein, aber wir wissen nicht, was.

Die Zeit vergeht wie im Flug, aber man benötigt Zeit, sie zu durchleben. Die Zeit vergeht nicht gleichmäßig, und ich wollte ein Gefühl dafür bekommen – dass die Zeit nicht klar umrissen ist. [Die Figuren] altern mit unterschiedlicher Geschwindigkeit." Newton scheint im Laufe des Films nicht zu altern, die anderen Figuren aber sehr wohl.

Der Chemieprofessor Dr. Nathan Bryce entwickelt sich im Verlauf des Romans zu einer Art Detektiv. Er will herausfinden, was hinter World Enterprises und ihrem mysteriösen Eigentümer steckt, wird leitender Chemiker des Raumschiffprojekts und horcht Betty Jo und Newton aus, um seinen Verdacht zu bestätigen, dass Newton ein Außerirdischer ist. Mayersberg: „Man findet Elemente aus fast jedem Genre, selbst aus dem Western. Das rührt teilweise daher, dass ein Aspekt der Geschichte zu einem anderen führt (Rätsel – Aufdeckung – Science-Fiction), und teils daher, dass der Film in Amerika spielt und von Amerika handelt. Und Amerika ist die Heimat all dieser Genres."

Mehrmals wird in Tevis' Roman das Gemälde *Landschaft mit dem Sturz des Ikarus* erwähnt (von dem man heute weiß, dass es sich um eine gute frühe Kopie eines Originals von Pieter Bruegel dem Älteren handelt) sowie W. H. Audens Gedicht über dieses Bild. Mayersberg: „Das Geniale an diesem Gemälde ist, dass niemand den Sturz des Ikarus bemerkt. Das fiel auch Auden auf und baute darauf sein Gedicht auf." Sowohl das Gemälde als auch das Gedicht werden in dem Film gezeigt, und den Zuschauern bleibt ausreichend Zeit, Letzteres zu lesen. „Schaut man sich die untere rechte Ecke [des Gemäldes] an, entdeckt man eine kleine Figur, die ins Wasser gefallen ist." Das Gemälde impliziert die Gleichgültigkeit des Menschen gegenüber dem Leid. „Was uns daran faszinierte, war

FROM SEVEN-UP
7up
CATCH-22
SKY SHOW PLANE

die Vorstellung, dass ihn niemand gesehen hat, weil jeder seinen eigenen Angelegenheiten nachging und in Gedanken mit anderen Dingen beschäftigt war. Daher ersannen wir eine mysteriöse Figur, die oben auf der Abraumhalde sitzt und nur zuschaut. Newton behauptet später, niemand habe seine Ankunft beobachtet, aber er wurde von jemandem gesehen. Der Beobachter taucht bis ganz zum Ende des Films, als Newton eingesperrt wird, nicht wieder auf. Der Mann hat jetzt übrigens einen Bart, und er ist offenbar ein Mensch, denn während Newton ja nicht gealtert ist, ist diese merkwürdige Gestalt, wie alle anderen, älter geworden. Wer ist dieser Mann? Er ist der Zuschauer und – meiner Ansicht nach – der Autor des Stückes, und er hat Newton die ganze Zeit beobachtet."

Der Roman war in einer Zukunft angesiedelt, in der sich afrikanische Staaten zur Abschreckung gegenseitig mit Kernwaffen bedrohen. Diese wachsende Gefahr eines Atomkriegs – Tevis hatte im Oktober die 13-tägige Kubakrise miterlebt – ist einer der Gründe für Newtons Anwesenheit auf der Erde. Er baut ein Raumschiff, um Treibstoff auf seinen Heimatplaneten Anthea zu schicken, damit die rund 300 überlebeden Antheaner zur Erde reisen und sie retten können, denn in der Vergangenheit hatten die Antheaner sich gegenseitig und beinahe auch ihren Planeten in einem schrecklichen Konflikt vernichtet. Nachdem die CIA Newton inhaftiert und seine wahre Identität aufgedeckt hat, gibt er sein Vorhaben auf und versinkt in Trunkenheit und Selbstvergessenheit.

Statt Newtons Plan zu erklären, deuten Mayersberg und Roeg in ihrem Drehbuch nur an, dass Newton beabsichtigt, Wasser nach Hause zu schicken, um seine Familie und seinen namenlosen Heimatplaneten zu retten. Der Schwerpunkt lag für die Autoren woanders. Zu Beginn des Romans beschreibt Tevis Newton als menschliches Wesen, das zwar nicht im eigentlichen Sinne ein Mensch, jedoch ebenso empfänglich für Liebe, Angst, starken körperlichen Schmerz und Selbstmitleid sei. Im Roman wird gezeigt, wie die Angst, entdeckt zu werden, in Verbindung mit dem starken körperlichen Schmerz, den das Leben auf unserem Planeten ihm verursacht (die Auswirkungen der Schwerkraft, die Verdauung der Nahrung, die Verletzungsgefahr durch selbst leichteste Berührung), so viel Druck auf Newton ausübt, dass er zusammenbricht und Trost in der Ginflasche findet. In seinem Leben fehlen Sex (da er nicht im eigentlichen Sinne *ein Mensch* ist) und Liebe.

Mayersberg: „Im Buch war die Beziehung zwischen Newton und Betty Jo im Wesentlichen platonisch. Das mag für ihn funktioniert haben – Außerirdische wissen schließlich nicht, wie Sex auf der Erde abläuft –,für sie jedoch nicht, denn sie wusste das ja verdammt gut. Das war etwas, worauf Nic näher eingehen wollte, weil geschlechtliche Beziehungen Gefahr bedeuten. Solange man niemanden berührt, geht es einem gut. In dem Augenblick, in dem man berührt und weitergeht, beginnt die Gefahr. Sex ist wie Alkohol: Hat man einmal damit angefangen, kann man nur schwer aufhören. Man gewöhnt sich daran und möchte mehr davon."

Betty Jo wurde in Mary-Lou umgetauft, und die Rolle wurde mit Candy Clark besetzt. Candy Clark: „Mary-Lou war ein junges, treuherziges Mädchen, das aus einer sehr kleinen Stadt kam. Sie war auf der Suche nach Liebe und fühlte sich sofort zu Thomas Jerome Newton hingezogen, weil er eine zerbrechliche, hilfsbedürftige Person war, und sie war ebenfalls hilfsbedürftig, weil sie allein war."

Roeg: „Die älteste Frage eines Verliebten ist: ‚Woran denkst du, Liebling?' und dann: ‚Woran denkst du wirklich?' Mary-Lou und Newton waren schon eine Weile zusammen, aber obwohl sie ihn etwas merkwürdig

fand, hatte sie keine Ahnung, woher er kam. Als sie ihm sagt, er könne offen zu ihr sein – was im menschlichen Kontext bedeutet: ‚Du kannst mir alles sagen, und ich liebe dich immer noch' –, zeigt er ihr [, dass er ein Außerirdischer ist, und] seine Art des Liebesakts: den Austausch von Körperflüssigkeiten. Das schreckt sie natürlich ab."

Nathan Bryce (gespielt von Rip Torn) wurde zu einem geschiedenen Professor umgeschrieben, der es mit Studentinnen treibt, bevor er mit den Nachforschungen über World Enterprises und Newton beginnt. Als sich Newton und Bryce kennenlernen, entwickelt sich eine Freundschaft zwischen ihnen, obwohl sie bereits eine übersinnliche Verbindung zu haben scheinen, denn bevor sie sich treffen, kann Newton Bryce „hören", und Newton „erscheint" Bryce sogar beim Angeln. Mayersberg: „Wir wollten etwas Übersinnliches hineinbringen. Newton ist weit voraus – er weiß, was Bryce denkt. Newton weiß, dass er entlarvt werden wird, und sagt zu≈Bryce: ‚Sei nicht misstrauisch. Hab keine Angst!' Es geht darum, was andere Leute machen, die mit der Tatsache konfrontiert werden, dass Newton alles bereits vorher weiß."

Bryce missbraucht Newtons Vertrauen, indem er heimlich eine Röntgenaufnahme von ihm anfertigt, die seine fremdartige Physiologie zum Vorschein bringt. Bowie: „Für mich ist der Film nach wie vor eine Geschichte über Verrat im Science-Fiction-Gewand. Der Augenblick, in dem Newton bewusst wird, dass Bryce die Aufnahmen gemacht hat, geht zurück auf die biblische Geschichte von Jesus, der weiß, dass er von Judas verraten werden wird. Auch Newton weiß, dass er verraten wird. Es ist ziemlich offensichtlich. Aber er tut einfach nichts dagegen."

Als Newton das Raumschiff erprobt hat und kurz vor der Abreise steht, greift die Regierung ein und entführt ihn. Newtons Fahrer liefert ihn aus, und Mary-Lou nimmt Geld dafür an, dass sie ihn verlässt. Mayersberg: „Der Punkt ist: Jeder verrät Newton, denn wenn du diese Fähigkeit hast und diese Macht, dann will jeder etwas von dir. Sie wollen Geld. Als die Behörde kommt, um Farnsworth aus dem Fenster zu werfen, dann nur deshalb, weil er zu viel Macht über seine Firma hat. Die Regierung möchte die Finanzen steuern können. Was uns interessierte, war die Vorstellung einer fehlenden Trennung von Wirtschaft und Politik, und ich denke, da hatten wir eine ziemlich gute Vorahnung. Ein Konzern übernimmt einen anderen – die Tatsache, dass einer der beiden Konzerne der Staat ist, spielt keine Rolle."

Bryce lebt anschließend mit Mary-Lou zusammen – das ist seine Art des Verrats. Clark: „Mary-Lou konnte Nathan Bryce nie wirklich lieben, weil sie immer noch auf Newton fixiert war, und so hatten sie diese Beziehung, die nie harmonisch war. Und Thomas Jerome Newton kam nie darüber hinweg, dass er seine Frau und seine Kinder auf dem anderen Planeten zurückgelassen hatte. So sehnt er sich noch immer nach dem Unerreichbaren, wie auch Mary-Lou sich nach Newton verzehrt. Niemand bekommt, was er will."

Rip Torn: „Das Tragische an Newtons Leben ist, dass er versagt hat. Er war nicht in der Lage, seine Zivilisation zu retten. Er war nicht in der Lage, seine Familie zu retten. Dies ist die Geschichte von Menschen, deren Zug längst abgefahren ist, die aber immer weitermachen."

## PRODUKTION

Nachdem Bowie im Boot war, präsentierte Roeg das Drehbuch verschiedenen Studios und nahm schließlich ein Angebot von Michael Deeley bei British Lion

an. Das Studio, dessen Geschichte bis ins Jahr 1927 zurückreichte – sein illustres Portfolio umfasste Klassiker wie *Der dritte Mann* (1949), *Herr der Fliegen* (1963) und *The Wicker Man* (1973) –, befand sich damals in einer prekären finanziellen Situation. Die Zusicherung von Paramount – dem Verleih von Roegs letztem Film *Wenn die Gondeln Trauer tragen* (1973) –, 1,5 Millionen Dollar für die US-Rechte zu zahlen, ermöglichte British Lion jedoch einen Bankkredit.

Im Unterschied zum Roman enthält der Film Szenen, die auf Newtons Heimatplaneten spielen. Für diese Sequenzen brauchte man eine ausgedörrte Landschaft, die obendrein in der Nähe eines Flughafens liegen sollte, damit man das belichtete Filmmaterial jeden Tag nach Los Angeles fliegen, dort entwickeln und zur Begutachtung zurück zu Roeg transportieren konnte. Die Wahl fiel schließlich auf Albuquerque in New Mexico als Basislager. Für Roeg besitzt „New Mexico … einen gewissen mystischen Charme, der mir vorher nicht bewusst gewesen war", und Mayersberg ergänzt: „Dort gibt es mehr Ufo- und Alien-Sichtungen als im gesamten Rest der Welt zusammengenommen." New Mexico ist der Standort von White Sands, dem Testgelände von NASA und Militär und Schauplatz der ersten Atombombenversuche im Jahr 1945, und in der Nähe der Kleinstadt Roswell soll es 1947 zum Absturz eines Ufos gekommen sein. Produzent Michael Deeley sah noch weitere Vorteile: „Es lag außerhalb des Blickfelds der Filmgewerkschaften, und da [Albuquerque] damals keine allzu wohlhabende Stadt war, waren wir und die Tatsache, dass wir unser Geld dort ausgaben, sehr willkommen. Es gab ein neues Hilton-Hotel, in dem der Stab für 15 Dollar pro Person und Nacht wohnen konnte und wo wir unsere Lkw parken durften. Hätte ich die Crew in Hollywood angeheuert, wäre es so teuer geworden, dass wir es uns nicht hätten leisten können, also entschlossen wir uns, das Risiko einzugehen. Jedes einzelne Mitglied des Stabes ging zur US-Botschaft am Londoner Grosvenor Square und beantragte ein Besuchervisum. Wir charterten ein Flugzeug von Aer Lingus und luden so viel Ausrüstung ein, wie wir tragen konnten, während die gesamte Filmcrew bereits an Bord war, und dann flogen wir nach Albuquerque. Zwei Tage später begannen wir mit den Dreharbeiten. Das war das erste – und bis in alle Zeiten vermutlich letzte – Mal, dass eine komplett britische Crew einen ganzen Spielfilm in den USA drehte."

„Ich war zum ersten Mal in Amerika. Ich war begeistert und bin es noch", erinnert sich der Standbildfotograf David James und spricht damit wohl auch seinen Kollegen aus dem Herzen. Bowie und sein Freund Geoff MacCormack (der als Bowies Backgroundsänger unter dem Namen Warren Peace auftrat) reisten mit dem Zug von Los Angeles nach Albuquerque an und übernachteten ebenfalls im Hilton. James: „Der größte Teil der englischen Crew wohnte in dem Hotel, und ein paar mieteten sich eigene Unterkünfte. Nic drehte gerne im ersten Tageslicht, also standen wir normalerweise um sechs oder halb sieben auf und fuhren zum Set, um dort zu frühstücken. Wir bekamen Tagesdispositionen, und die meisten von uns hatten Autos, mit denen wir selbst zu den Drehorten fahren konnten. New Mexico am Morgen war wunderschön, der Himmel war klar und die Sonne noch nicht aufgegangen. Die Stimmung war gesellig, und beim Frühstück verglichen wir mitunter die Intensität unserer Kater. Schließlich kamen auch Nic und der DP [*director of photography* = Chefkameramann Anthony Richmond] und bereiteten den Drehort für den Tag vor. Nach und nach kreuzten die Schauspieler auf und probten."

Die elfwöchigen Dreharbeiten begannen am Montag, dem 2. Juni 1975 in Los Lunas – Roeg hielt den Ortsnamen (schlechtes Spanisch für „die Monde") für ein

gutes Omen – damit, dass Newton nach Haneyville hineinspaziert, einen goldenen Ring verkauft und Wasser aus dem Rio Grande trinkt. James: „Wir trödelten nicht herum. Wir arbeiteten sehr zügig an den Aufbauten."

Als Newton in die Stadt kommt, läuft er an einem verlassenen Rummelplatz vorbei und wird von einem Betrunkenen angepöbelt. Bowie: „Das Erste, was Newton in Zusammenhang mit einem Menschen sieht, sind die Auswirkungen des Alkohols, der ihn schließlich zerstören oder zumindest hier festhalten wird." Dann kommt eine kräftige Windböe und reißt einen Ballon in die Luft. Roeg: „Der Ballon riss sich los und hüpfte auf uns zu. Ich gab Anweisung, nicht abzubrechen, sondern weiterzudrehen."

James: „Fats Domino kam mit seiner Band ins Hilton, und dank David saßen Geoff MacCormack und ich in der ersten Reihe." Sie tranken eine stattliche Menge Budweiser. Geoff MacCormack: „Als Neunjährige hatten David und ich uns *Blueberry Hill* gekauft, und so freuten wir uns wirklich darauf, den Mann live spielen zu sehen. Anschließend torkelten wir hinter die Bühne.
Wir klopften an die Tür des Dicken, und von innen schallte eine dröhnende Stimme: ‚Wer ist da?' – ‚David Bowie.' – ‚Wer?' – ‚David Bowie aus London.' – ‚David *wer*?'" Ein paar Mädchen klopften an die Tür und wurden sofort hereingelassen. Bowie versuchte es noch einmal. „Die Tür öffnete sich, und da stand, auf uns herabschauend, der größte schwarze Mann, den ich je gesehen hatte. Er teilte uns mit, dass Mr Domino im Augenblick beschäftigt sei, und schlug uns die Tür ins Gesicht. David sah diesen Vorfall nicht als Affront. Im Gegenteil: Es war einfach zu lustig." James: „Anschließend gingen wir mit ein paar Bandmitgliedern ins Café, und Bowie tanzte auf den Tischen. Die Frauen in dem Café schrien ihn an, er solle von den Tischen herunterkommen, sonst würden sie die Polizei rufen. ‚Ruft sie nur! Ruft sie nur!', forderte Bowie sie heraus."

MacCormack: „Nachdem er eine Zeit lang im Hilton gewohnt hatte, mietete David bei Santa Fe einen Bungalow an, und seine PA [persönliche Assistentin] Coco [Schwab] und ich zogen mit ihm dort ein. David nutzte den hellen Wintergarten, um wieder mit dem Malen zu beginnen." In Drehpausen arbeitete Bowie an neuen Songs, Geschichten und an seiner geplanten Autobiografie *The Return of the Thin White Duke.*

Das Hotel Artesia in Artesia war ein wichtiger Drehort. Der größte Teil des Hotels war ungenutzt, sodass das Team freie Hand hatte, Wände einzureißen und Zimmer nach eigenen Bedürfnissen umzugestalten. Das Hotel wurde nicht nur für Newtons Ankunft im Hotel, die Fahrstuhlszene und die Hotelzimmerszenen mit Mary-Lou genutzt, sondern auch als Ort, an dem Newton von der Regierung gefangen gehalten wird.

James: „Nic entwarf ein Set und stellte dann die Charaktere hinein. Das war seine Art von Zauberei. Sie probten. Sie gingen die Dialoge durch und nahmen hier und da notwendige Veränderungen vor. Anschließend ließ Nic sie die Szene proben und legte die Kamerapositionen fest. Bei den Dreharbeiten sprach er leise und ließ stets seinen dezenten britischen Sinn für Humor durchblitzen."

Clark: „David war nicht der Typ, der über seine Gefühle sprach, daher wusste man nie, was in ihm vorging. Außerdem verbrachte er seine Zeit ausschließlich mit seinem eigenen Gefolge. Außerhalb der Dreharbeiten aßen wir also niemals gemeinsam oder verbrachten die arbeitsfreie Zeit miteinander. Er war sehr entrückt und still, und das war für mich natürlich perfekt, weil die Figur, die ich spielte, nie wusste, was in Thomas Newton vorging."

Bowie: „Es war der erste [Film], den ich je gedreht habe. Ich kannte mich nicht aus mit den üblichen Abläufen [einer Filmproduktion], daher verließ ich

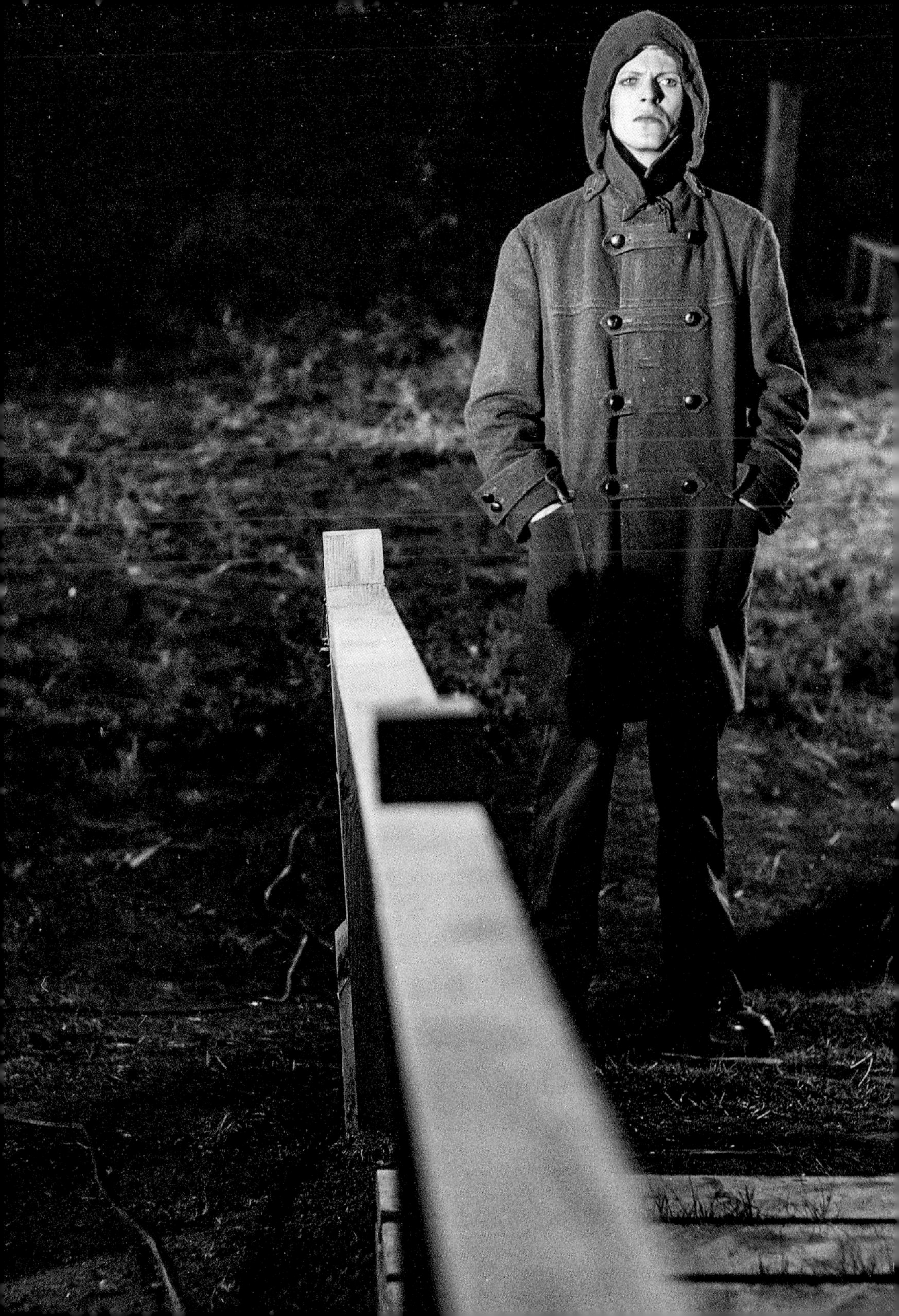

mich weitgehend auf meine Instinkte, und die waren ziemlich zügellos. Ich lernte einfach meinen Text für den Tag und lieferte ihn so ab, wie es mein Gefühl mir sagte. Ich fühlte mich tatsächlich so entfremdet wie die Figur. Es war eine ziemlich natürliche Darbietung … eine gute Zurschaustellung von jemandem, der buchstäblich vor deinen Augen zerfällt. Ich war völlig unsicher und nahm etwa zehn Gramm [Kokain] am Tag. Ich war von Anfang bis Ende völlig stoned."

Szenenbildner Brian Eatwell baute eine Außenkulisse für Newtons Haus im japanischen Stil am Ufer des Fenton Lake, der knapp 130 Kilometer nördlich von Albuquerque im Jemez-Gebirge und westlich von Los Alamos, dem Stützpunkt des Manhattan-Projekts, liegt. (Die Innenaufnahmen des Hauses mit seinen Wänden aus runden Lehmziegeln, damit sich Newton nicht verletzte, entstanden in Santa Fe.) Am gegenüberliegenden Seeufer wurde die Hütte des Parkaufsehers in Nathan Bryce' Haus verwandelt.

Im See gab es Forellen. James: „Rip Torn und ich teilten die Leidenschaft fürs Fliegenfischen. Eines Abends, als wir auf dem hölzernen Steg am See drehten, machten die Kameraleute und ein paar Einheimische nach Drehschluss ein kleines Lagerfeuer und setzten einen Topf mit Wasser auf. Rip brachte uns bei, wie man Krebse fängt. Wir fingen sie, warfen sie in den Topf und aßen sie."

Bowie: „Ich liebte Rip. Er war ein wundervoller Kerl. Er hatte was von Hemingway oder Mailer. Er besaß eine tolle männliche Art. Jeder Tag und jede Nacht waren ein riesiges Abenteuer für Rip. Jeden Morgen warteten wir gebannt darauf, von seinen Heldentaten zu hören. ‚Ich erzähl euch, was letzte Nacht passiert ist …', fing er an. Er kletterte über Stacheldrahtzäune und fiel in Gräben.

Eines Tages kam Rip besonders übel gelaunt zum Set. Aus irgendeinem Grund war er nicht gut auf Nic zu sprechen und knurrte: ‚Wenn Sie mich wie einen Hund behandeln, dann werde ich wie ein Hund reagieren.' Nic schaute ihn an, sagte zum Kameramann: ‚Heute drehen wir nicht mit Mr Torn', und ließ diesen schnaubend am Set stehen."

White Sands bei Alamogordo diente als Kulisse für den fremden Planeten. Bowie, Clark und zwei Kinderschauspieler mimten die außerirdische Familie. Sie trugen hautenge Anzüge, die von einem feinen Netz aus Schläuchen überzogen waren, die mit kostbarem Wasser gefüllt waren. Das auffälligste Merkmal der Außerirdischen waren ihre katzenartigen Augen. Bowie: „Damals bestanden Kontaktlinsen noch meist aus hartem Kunststoff und schmerzten wirklich außerordentlich in den Augen. Ich war wahnsinnig dehydriert, und die Wüste war auch nicht hilfreich." Roeg: „Als sich Candy ihre Kontaktlinsen anpassen ließ, saugte sich die Linse einfach an ihrem Augapfel fest. Sie passte zu gut. Es dauerte über eine Stunde, bis der Arzt herausgefunden hatte, wie er die Linse wieder herausbekommt."

Im gesamten Film gibt es visuelle und textuelle Verweise auf Eisenbahnen, die an Newtons Abschied von seiner Familie erinnern, die er per Zug verließ. Um diese Szene darzustellen, ließ Brian Eatwell in der Wüste Gleise für eine Einschienenbahn verlegen und gestaltete aus einem alten Traktor einen außerirdischen Zug. Der Zug hatte eine organische Oberfläche und war mit Sonnensegeln ausgestattet. Bowie: „Als der Zug auftauchte, entsprach er überhaupt nicht dem, was sich Nic vorgestellt hatte. Er lief im Gesicht erst blau an, dann rot und dann weiß und sagte: ‚Was ist das denn?' – ‚Das ist Ihr Zug, Sir.' – ‚Das ist kein Zug, das ist ein verfickter Hundezwinger!' Aber wir lebten

damit." Der Dreh wurde durch eine Panne des Traktors noch weiter erschwert. Da keine Ersatzteile zur Hand waren, brachte man Seile an dem „Zug" an und ließ ihn von Pferden aus dem Bild ziehen. James: „Solche Probleme sind beim Film normal."

Nach zehn Drehwochen in New Mexico zog die Produktion für die letzten paar Drehtage nach Los Angeles um. James: „Wir mussten es wegen der Gewerkschaften in L.A. und der Arbeitsgenehmigungen heimlich tun." Bowie mietete ein Haus in Bel-Air und verbrachte drehfreie Tage mit Musikaufnahmen in den Cherokee Studios.

Bei Tower Records am Sunset Strip kauft ein in die Jahre gekommener Bryce eine Schallplatte von The Visitor („Der Besucher" alias Newton). Im Hintergrund werden Exemplare von Bowies Album *Young Americans* zum Verkauf angeboten. Ebenfalls am Sunset, in einem japanischen Restaurant, wurde die Szene gefilmt, in der Newton die Kabuki-Theatervorstellung verlässt, weil ihn die Gewalt entsetzt. Auch die Aufnahmen zum letzten Treffen zwischen Bryce und Newton fanden am Sunset statt: im Restaurant Butterfield's. Roeg: „Das Geschäft wird dermaßen von wirtschaftlichen Faktoren bestimmt, dass man geneigt ist zu glauben, alles verlaufe linear. In der ersten Szene passiert Newton einen Rummelplatz. Als wir gerade vorbeigingen, setzte sich ein alter Penner in einem der Fahrgeschäfte auf und rülpste. So etwas hätten wir auf keinen Fall planen können. Das erste menschliche Geräusch in dem Film ist ein Rülpsen und das letzte auch, als Bowie an seinem Tisch rülpst. Mir gefällt die Vorstellung vom Zufall. Man muss die verschiedenen Dinge wahrnehmen, die sich um einen herum abspielen, wenn man dreht. Was Gott zum Lachen bringt, sind Menschen, die Pläne schmieden."

## NACHBEARBEITUNG

Roeg kehrte nach Großbritannien zurück, um den Film mit Graeme Clifford zu schneiden. Deeley: „Ursprünglich sollte David Bowie die Musik für den Film liefern." Bowie: „Ich verbrachte zwei oder drei Monate damit, Teile des Materials zusammenzustellen." Roeg lehnte die Kompositionen, die er ablieferte, jedoch ab. Paul Buckmaster, ein Cellist, der Bowies *Space Oddity* arrangiert hatte, arbeitete mit Bowie an den Nummern und kann sich denken, woran es scheiterte: „Erstens war er den Ansprüchen an Komposition und Darbietung, die für einen guten Film erforderlich sind, nicht gewachsen. Zweitens glaube ich, dass es nicht gut zu dem Film passte. Und drittens war es nicht wirklich das, wonach Nic Roeg suchte." Deeley: „Nics Cutter Graeme Clifford wollte dann ein paar Nummern von Pink Floyd verwenden, aber die standen nicht zur Verfügung und wären eh viel zu teuer gewesen. Am Ende stellte John Phillips – ehemals bei The Mamas and the Papas – eine Kombination aus ein paar neuen und ein paar existierenden Aufnahmen zusammen." Tatsächlich hatte Phillips Bowies Filmmusik gehört und beschrieb sie später als „eindringlich und schön, mit Röhrenglockenspiel, japanischen Schellen und etwas, was sich nach elektronischem Wind und Wellenschlag anhörte". Diese Beschreibung könnte auch auf die sechs Tracks des japanischen Prog-Rock-Komponisten Stomu Yamashta zutreffen, die an Schlüsselstellen des Films zum Einsatz kamen. Im Hinblick auf Bowies Demos erklärt der Komponist: „Einige flossen in *Station to Station* ein, andere wurden zum Album *Low*, das ich ein paar Jahre später mit Brian Eno in Berlin einspielte."

Deeley: „Während die Musik sorgfältig eingearbeitet wurde, brachte ich einen Rohschnitt nach New York, um ihn dem neu ernannten Vorsitzenden von Paramount

Pictures, Barry Diller, vorzuführen. Nach der Sichtung sollte Paramount die erste Zahlung an uns im Rahmen des Vertrags mit British Lion veranlassen. Nachdem das Licht wieder angeschaltet worden war, sagte Diller ein paar Minuten lang gar nichts. Schließlich meinte er: ‚Das ist nicht der Film, den Paramount gekauft hat. Der Film, den wir gekauft haben, ist linear, dieser hier ist es nicht', und er deutete an, dass er den Vertrag nicht zu erfüllen gedachte, den seine Firma vor seiner Ernennung abgeschlossen hatte. Das hätte für British Lion eine Katastrophe bedeutet. Kein anderer US-Verleih würde *Der Mann, der vom Himmel fiel* übernehmen wollen, weil er durch Paramounts Ablehnung automatisch ein Ladenhüter wäre. Hollywood ist da äußerst abergläubisch."

Schließlich zahlte Don Rugoff von Cinema V einen Vorschuss von 850.000 Dollar für den Verleih in den USA.

## KINOSTART

*Der Mann, der vom Himmel fiel* wurde am 18. März 1976 im Londoner Leicester Square Theatre uraufgeführt. Der Film erhielt gemischte Kritiken. Roeg: „Ein Kritiker beschwerte sich über den Satz: ‚Alle Dinge beginnen und enden in der Ewigkeit.' Ich sagte zu ihm: ‚Ihnen ist schon klar, dass das [William] Blake ist?'" Wenn man den Film zum ersten Mal sieht, ist es aufgrund des elliptischen Schnittschemas schwer, den verschiedenen Handlungsfäden, Bildmotiven und Themen zu folgen, die den Film zusammenhalten. Roeg hatte die Grammatik der filmischen Erzählung grundlegend verändert, indem er „die Krücke der Zeit fortnahm, an der sich das Publikum üblicherweise festhält. Ich denke, der Film ist eher wie ein Leben, das aus vielen einzelnen Episoden besteht. Am Ende eines Lebens fällt es schwer, den eigentlichen Handlungsfaden zu finden."

Roeg wollte, dass das Publikum „die Leinwand liest" und den Film „auf sich wirken" lässt.

Cinema V brachte den Film am 28. Mai in die amerikanischen Kinos, machte aber von seinem Kürzungsrecht Gebrauch. Der Film wurde um 20 Minuten geschnitten, worüber Roeg „völlig erschüttert und entsetzt" war. Die Kritiken waren auch hier gemischt.

Im Laufe der letzten 40 Jahre hat der Film an Ansehen gewonnen – nicht zuletzt auch deshalb, weil Roegs damals bahnbrechende filmische Erzählweise inzwischen von zahlreichen Filmemachern übernommen wurde und das Publikum gelernt hat, „die Leinwand zu lesen". Bowie: „Mich reizte die Idee der Fragmentierung schon, weil ich ein ziemlicher Fan von William S. Burroughs' Schnitttechnik war. Nic war klar, dass zwei Dinge, die aufeinandertreffen, ein drittes Stück Information bilden können, das niemandem von uns bewusst war, und es freute ihn, wenn er sah, wie diese Zufälle einen Sinn ergaben, aus dem Chaos Ordnung entstand. Die Ordnung im Chaos ist heutzutage eine wesentliche Theorie in der Physik. Ich griff dieses Element auf und verwendete es in einem großen Teil meiner späteren Arbeit, und ich nehme an, es erreichte seinen Zenit in meiner Zusammenarbeit mit Brian Eno. Diese Erfahrung von Koinzidenz und Fragmentierung, die ich bei den Dreharbeiten mit Nic machte, hat mein weiteres Werk definitiv geprägt."

Am Ende des Films spürt Bryce Newton durch eine Schallplatte von The Visitor auf: „Poesie und Musik, wie du sie nie zuvor gehört hast." „Hat sie dir gefallen?", fragt Newton. „Nicht sehr", erwidert Bryce. „Nun", meint Newton, „ich habe sie ja auch nicht für dich gemacht." Newton hofft vergebens, dass sie im Radio gespielt wird und so eines Tages seine Familie erreichen könnte, die er zurückließ. Aber Roeg versteht die wirkliche Tragik der Situation, die vielleicht der Grund für Newtons Schmerz ist: „Er ist kein Besucher mehr. Er ist einer von uns."

CANADA DRY
TONIC
WATER

20 1 18 4 13 6 10 15 2 17 3 19 7 16 8 11 14 9 12 5

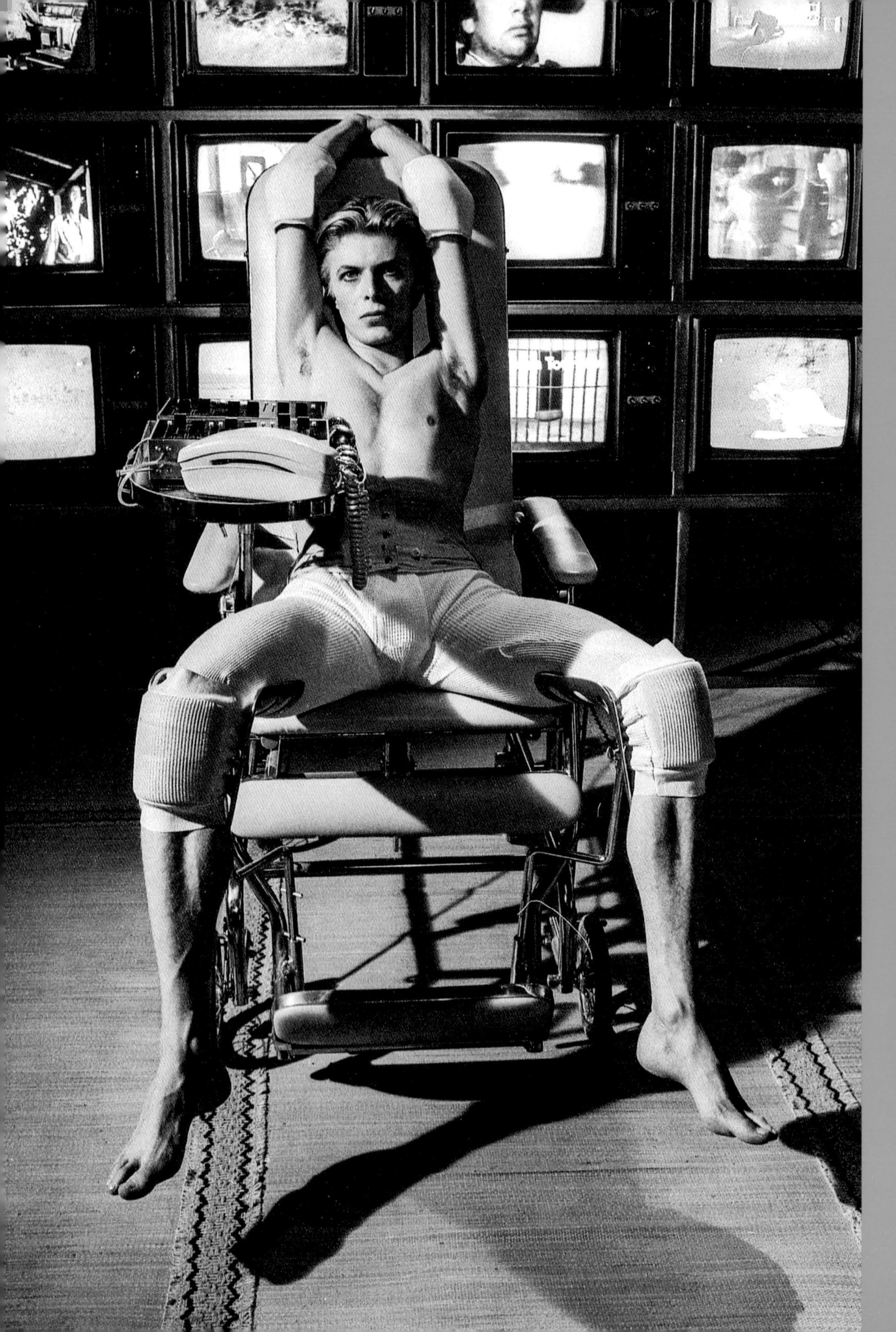

# *LA CHUTE*

Par Paul Duncan

Une limousine noire lacère un morne paysage désertique. Sur la banquette arrière, un David Bowie très mince, pâle et fragile – ses cheveux orange et blonds dépassant de son chapeau – boit du lait à même la brique et parle de sa tournée *Diamond Dogs*. Bowie sillonne alors l'Amérique du Nord depuis juin 1974 pour faire la promotion de son album et jouer des morceaux comme « Space Oddity », « Rebel Rebel » et « Changes ». Après une pause en août, consacrée à l'enregistrement de plusieurs titres soul pour son prochain album, *Young Americans*, Bowie a repris sa tournée jusqu'en décembre, en limousine noire parce qu'il refuse de prendre l'avion. Interrogé sur sa tournée américaine et sur la nouvelle musique qu'il est en train de créer, Bowie regarde à l'intérieur de sa brique de lait : « Il y a une mouche qui flotte dans mon lait, et c'est un corps étranger. C'est un peu comme ça que je me sens. Je suis un corps étranger ici, et je n'ai pas pu m'empêcher d'absorber ce dans quoi je baigne. Cela a comblé un besoin en moi. C'est devenu une terre mythique. » Il continue : « Il y a un malaise sous-jacent [en Amérique]. Ils ont développé un calme superficiel pour minimiser l'énorme pression qu'ils s'imposent ici. » Bowie ressent aussi un malaise sous-jacent dans son propre travail. Il a créé Major Tom, Ziggy Stardust et Aladdin Sane : « Ils sont tous des facettes de moi ; à un moment, je me suis perdu. Je n'arrivais pas à décider si j'écrivais des personnages ou si les personnages m'écrivaient, ou si nous étions tous une seule et même personne. »

Le réalisateur Nicolas Roeg a vu le documentaire pris sur le vif *Cracked Actor* d'Alan Yentob (diffusé par la BBC au Royaume-Uni le 26 janvier 1975) et travaille avec le scénariste Paul Mayersberg sur *L'Homme qui venait d'ailleurs*, une adaptation du roman de Walter Tevis *L'Homme tombé du ciel* (*The Man Who Fell to Earth*, 1963), à propos d'un extraterrestre grand, mince, aux cheveux blancs et aux os saillants, qui vient sur Terre, se baptise Thomas Jerome Newton, fait breveter un certain nombre d'avancées technologiques par l'intermédiaire de son avocat, Oliver Farnsworth, accumule des richesses, crée une société, World Enterprises, et construit un vaisseau spatial pour une raison quelconque, tout en demeurant un ermite, inconnu et coupé du monde, à l'exception de quelques personnes. Roeg a d'abord envisagé l'écrivain et réalisateur Michael Crichton (*Le Mystère Andromède*, *Mondwest* et plus tard *Jurassic Park*) pour le rôle de Newton parce qu'il mesurait plus de deux mètres, mais après avoir vu Bowie dans *Cracked Actor*, il se rend à l'évidence : « Je ne pouvais imaginer personne d'autre pour le rôle. Je ne connaissais pas David, mais j'avais vu son travail et c'est devenu une sorte d'obsession parce qu'il semblait exister des parallèles dans les attitudes de Bowie et dans la pensée qui guidait son travail à ce moment-là. »

"THE MAN WHO FELL TO EARTH"
DIRECTOR
NICOLAS ROEG
DIR. OF PHOTOGRAPHY
ANTHONY RICHMOND
SCENE
330
TAKE
1
INT
DATE
7-7-75

Roeg envoie immédiatement un script à Bowie et, en février, il part à New York pour le rencontrer. « J'ai appris que David avait envie de me voir. Il enregistrait mais devait avoir fini vers 21 h 30. Je suis arrivé chez lui et j'ai discuté avec des inconnus qui allaient et venaient. J'ai reçu un coup de fil me prévenant que ce serait plutôt 23 heures. Vers 3 heures du matin, je pensais qu'il n'arriverait plus. J'avais déjà pris plusieurs Martini, donc je me suis dit que quitte à avoir attendu jusqu'à 3 heures, je pouvais bien pousser jusqu'à 3 h 30. Il est arrivé vers 5 heures, et nous avons parlé cinq minutes. Il m'a dit : "Ne t'inquiète pas. Je vais le faire. Fais-moi savoir quand tu as besoin de moi, et j'arrive." Et il m'a reconduit à la porte. »

Bowie : « Je ne connaissais Nic que pour son travail avec Mick Jagger sur *Performance* [1970], donc j'ai regardé ses films précédents et j'ai été très impressionné, bouleversé, même, par son travail. *Walkabout* [1971] m'a particulièrement parlé. C'était un film merveilleux.

« J'étais sorti et quand je me suis souvenu de notre rendez-vous, j'avais déjà une heure de retard, alors je me suis dit "Oh, non, je l'ai manqué, il a dû partir", et j'ai pensé à autre chose. Quand j'ai fini par rentrer à la maison, j'ai trouvé Nic qui m'attendait très patiemment, assis dans ma cuisine. Huit heures de retard, et le gars m'avait attendu ! Une sacrée persévérance, n'est-ce pas ?

« Ce que je n'ai pas dit à Nic, c'est que je cherchais à écourter notre conversation au maximum parce que je ne voulais pas qu'il se rende compte que je n'avais pas lu le script. Il évoquait des passages du film et je faisais "Oui. Oui. Voilà. Absolument. Je vois ça". Je l'ai bluffé comme j'ai pu. »

Alors pourquoi Bowie a-t-il accepté de faire le film ? « C'est à la fois le fait d'avoir vu *Walkabout* et de rencontrer Nic en personne qui m'ont convaincu que c'était un projet auquel j'avais vraiment envie de participer. C'est sans doute la meilleure décision que j'ai prise à partir de rien, rien d'autre que le travail précédent du gars. »

## SCÉNARIO

Le premier roman de Walter Tevis, *L'Arnaqueur* (The Hustler, 1959), est devenu un best-seller après son adaptation au cinéma, en 1961, sous la direction de Robert Rossen, avec Paul Newman dans le rôle-titre. Le film fut nommé neuf fois aux Oscars et en remporta deux. C'est l'histoire du joueur de billard et arnaqueur « Fast Eddie » Felson, qui pouvait battre n'importe qui. Sauf lui-même.

« En apparence, *L'Arnaqueur* n'a pas grand-chose en commun avec *L'Homme qui venait d'ailleurs*, explique Mayersberg, mais à mon sens ils sont très proches. La société américaine aime les gagnants. Elle ne tolère pas les perdants, ceux qui n'atteignent pas leur but. Il y a une réplique dans *L'Arnaqueur* où Eddie entend une petite voix tout au fond de lui, qui dit : "Tu n'as pas à gagner à tout prix." Du point de vue de Tevis, il était plus important d'être le meilleur que de gagner. C'est aussi un élément crucial dans *L'Homme qui venait d'ailleurs*. Voilà un type qui est largement supérieur aux gens qui l'entourent, intellectuellement, scientifiquement, etc. et qui, pourtant, échoue. Je crois que l'idée de Tevis était que si vous avez des talents exceptionnels, le monde va se charger de vous le faire payer.

« L'autre aspect de *L'Arnaqueur* c'est le thème de l'ivresse. [Sarah Packard] est une intello alcoolique lorsqu'entre dans sa vie [Felson], un rustre glandeur qui se trouve être un surdoué du billard.

Dans *L'Homme qui venait d'ailleurs*, nous sommes en présence d'un génie, Thomas Jerome Newton, qui entre dans la vie d'une fille alcoolique sans aucune éducation [Betty Jo] qui ne comprend pas de quoi il parle. Il est venu sur Terre parce que sa planète est trop sèche. La première chose qu'il fait est de trouver de l'eau. Il ne va jamais quelque part s'il n'y a pas d'eau. Newton est assoiffé bien avant d'atterrir. Alors quand il rencontre cette femme et qu'elle lui propose du gin, cela lui va. Tout le monde boit – sans eau il n'y aurait pas de vie sur la planète – c'est l'essence de la vie. »

*L'Homme tombé du ciel* a fait l'objet de plusieurs projets d'adaptation dès sa sortie en librairie, en 1963. Mayersberg raconte : « Les droits d'adaptation avaient été acquis pour une série télévisée dans le style du *Fugitif* où chaque semaine les protagonistes devaient attraper cet extraterrestre, qui s'en sortait toujours. L'option a expiré parce qu'ils n'ont trouvé personne capable de l'adapter. C'était une tâche difficile parce qu'aucun budget ne permettait de faire tout ce qui est dans le livre, et puis il n'est pas un vrai héros, il n'a pas de pistolet laser, ce genre de choses.

« Nic m'a envoyé *L'Homme tombé du ciel* en 1974, et ce qui m'a frappé, c'est que ce n'était pas un roman de science-fiction conventionnel. Ce n'était pas, malgré de vagues similitudes, le *En terre étrangère* [*Stranger in a Strange Land*, 1961] de Robert Heinlein. Il n'y avait ni la machinerie ni la quincaillerie de la science-fiction. L'auteur utilisait un postulat typique de la science-fiction – un extraterrestre sur Terre – comme prétexte pour considérer les États-Unis de l'époque. Nous sommes partis de ce principe et nous avons présenté les États-Unis, visuellement surtout, d'un point de vue d'extraterrestre. Même s'il reste sur Terre des années, il a du mal à comprendre comme tout fonctionne. Nous nous sommes moins souciés d'où il venait, ou même de la raison de sa venue, que de la manière donc un habitant d'une autre planète verrait la nôtre. »

Roeg : « Ce n'est pas comme si j'avais lu le bouquin et que je m'étais dit : "On peut raconter cette histoire." Il m'est apparu comme un véhicule idéal pour aborder les comportements qui prévalaient à l'époque dans tellement d'aspects de nos vies. L'intrigue est essentielle, mais pour moi c'est une coquille habitée par les personnages. Toutes les intrigues de nos vies sont intéressantes. Mais la façon dont nous les habitons est plus intéressante encore. »

Dans leur adaptation, Mayersberg et Roeg dépouillent méthodiquement le roman jusqu'à l'os et le rebâtissent entièrement. Le roman, qui se déroule en 1985, 1988 et 1990, suit Newton qui court contre le temps pour construire son vaisseau spatial.

Roeg : « Nous ne voyons pas à quel point nous sommes liés par le temps dans nos vies. Lorsque nous écrivions le script avec Paul, c'est surprenant comme la question du temps revenait souvent sur le tapis ; j'ai décidé de supprimer tout ça. Il n'existe dans le film aucune mention du temps qui passe. Je voulais rompre avec la conception linéaire du temps en dissolvant et diluant les transitions d'un lieu à un autre, d'un personnage à un autre, ou la présence d'une même personne dans un lieu similaire ou différent. Il s'est peut-être passé des choses entre les plans, mais nous ignorons quoi. Le temps file mais la vie prend du temps. Le temps ne s'écoule pas de manière égale et je voulais transmettre cette notion – le temps n'est pas particulièrement délimité. Les différents moments que nous vivons vieillissent à des vitesses différentes. » Au cours du film, Newton semble d'ailleurs ne pas vieillir, contrairement aux autres personnages.

À mesure que le roman progresse, le Dr Nathan Bryce, un professeur de chimie, devient un genre de détective. Il se met à enquêter sur World Enterprises et son mystérieux propriétaire, obtient une place de chimiste dans l'entreprise, sur le projet de vaisseau spatial, et soutire subrepticement des informations à Betty Jo et Newton pour obtenir la confirmation que Newton est un extraterrestre. Mayersberg : « Le film contient des éléments de presque tous les genres, même du western, à cause de la façon dont les différents aspects de l'histoire sont reliés les uns aux autres (mystère, enquête, science-fiction) et parce que le film se passe en Amérique et parle de l'Amérique. Et l'Amérique est la terre natale de tous les genres. »

Le roman de Tevis se réfère plusieurs fois à *La Chute d'Icare*, une copie ancienne d'une toile de Bruegel l'Ancien, ainsi qu'au poème de W. H. Auden qui l'évoque. Mayersberg : « Ce qui est génial dans cette toile c'est que personne ne remarque Icare. C'est ce qu'observe Auden et c'est la base de son poème. » La toile et le poème figurent tous les deux dans le film, de façon que le public ait le temps de le lire. « Si vous regardez dans le coin inférieur droit, vous remarquerez un petit personnage qui vient de tomber à l'eau. » La toile évoque l'indifférence de l'humanité face à la souffrance. « Cette idée que personne ne l'a vu parce que chacun était occupé à ses petites affaires et avait d'autres choses en tête nous a intrigués. Alors nous avons incrusté un mystérieux personnage au sommet du terril, qui se contente de regarder. Newton raconte que personne ne l'a vu arriver, mais c'est faux. L'observateur ne réapparaît qu'à la toute fin, quand Newton est incarcéré. Cet homme porte alors la barbe et il est humain, puisqu'il a vieilli comme tous les personnages, à l'exception de Newton. Qui est cet homme ? Il est le témoin et, à mon sens, l'auteur de l'histoire, qui n'a jamais quitté Newton des yeux. »

Le roman se passe dans un avenir où les pays africains menacent d'utiliser l'arme nucléaire en guise de dissuasion. Cette menace grandissante d'un holocauste nucléaire – Tevis a vécu les treize jours de la crise des missiles cubains en octobre 1962, quand le monde s'est retrouvé au bord de la guerre nucléaire – est une des raisons pour lesquelles Newton est venu sur Terre. Il fait bâtir un vaisseau spatial pour envoyer du carburant sur sa planète d'origine, Anthéa, afin que les quelque trois cents Anthéens qui restent puissent à leur tour venir sur Terre et aider à la sauver – dans le passé, les Anthéens ont détruit leurs semblables et leur planète au cours d'un horrible conflit. Lorsque Newton est arrêté par la CIA et que son identité est découverte, il abandonne le projet et plonge dans l'oubli de soi alcoolique.

Plutôt que d'expliquer le plan de Newton, Mayersberg et Roeg distillent dans le script quelques indices qui laissent penser que Newton prévoit d'envoyer de l'eau pour sauver sa famille et sa planète, qui n'est pas nommée. Leur intérêt réside ailleurs.

Au début du roman, Tevis écrit à propos de Newton : « Il était humain ; mais il n'était pas vraiment un *homme*. Ainsi, comme tout humain, il était capable d'éprouver l'amour, la peur, l'intense douleur physique et l'apitoiement. » Le roman montre ensuite que la peur de la découverte et de l'échec, combinée à l'intense souffrance physique que provoque chez lui le fait de vivre sur Terre (effets de la gravité, digestion de la nourriture, douleur au moindre contact), inflige une telle pression à Newton qu'il craque et trouve le réconfort au fond d'une bouteille de gin. Ce qui manque à sa vie est le sexe (puisqu'il n'est pas un *homme*) et l'amour.

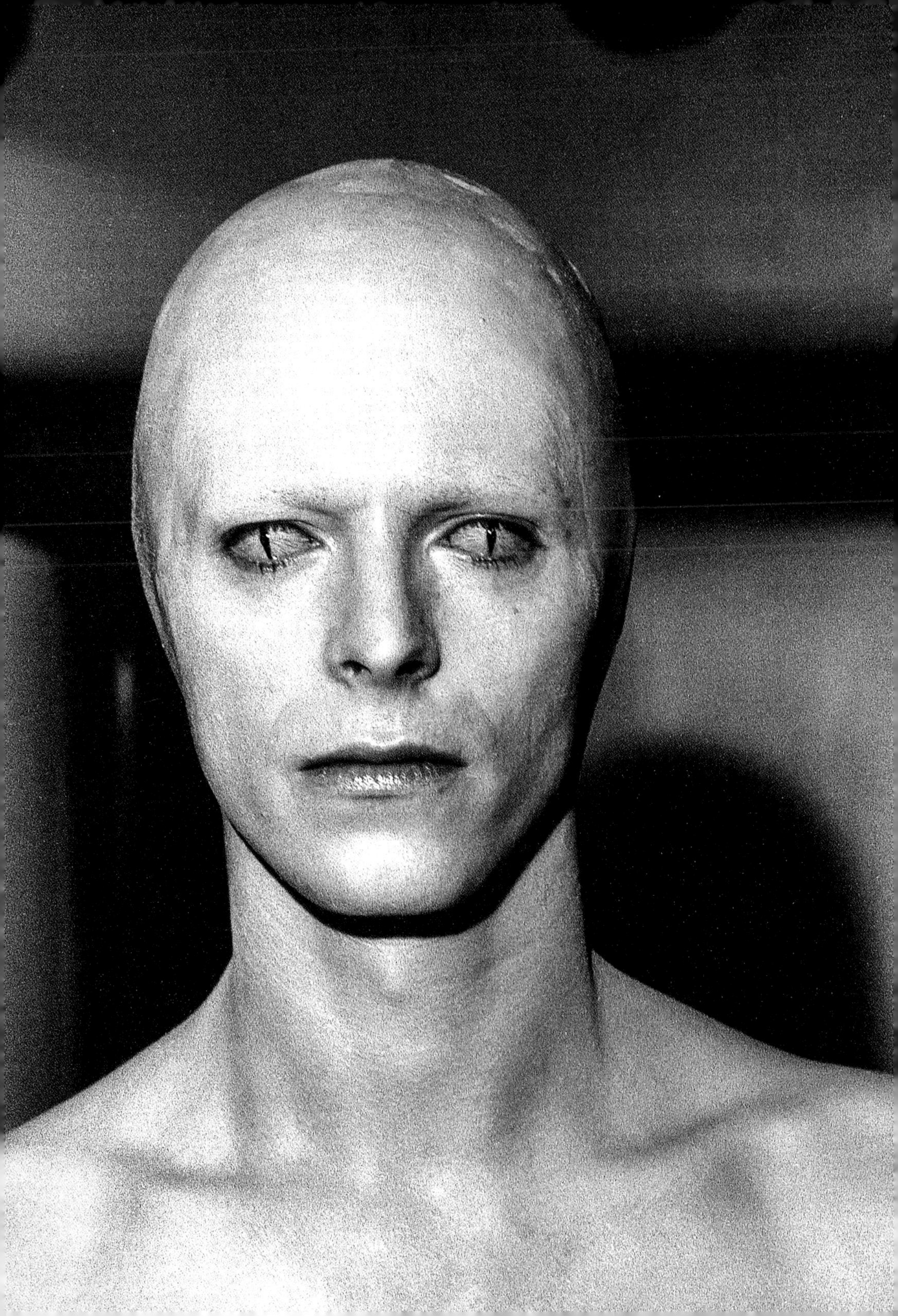

Mayersberg : « Dans le livre, la relation entre Newton et Betty Jo est essentiellement platonique. Ce n'est pas un problème pour lui – les aliens ne sont pas censés savoir comment fonctionne le sexe sur Terre – mais c'est un gros problème pour elle, qui sait oh ! combien ce qu'est le sexe. C'était un sujet que Nic souhaitait explorer parce que les relations sexuelles représentent le danger. Tant que vous ne touchez personne, tout va bien. À la minute où vous avancez sur cette voie, le danger entre en jeu. Le sexe est un autre alcool – une fois que vous avez commencé à boire, c'est très dur de vous arrêter. Vous vous y faites et vous en voulez toujours plus. »

Betty Jo fut rebaptisée Mary-Lou et Candy Clark engagée pour le rôle. Candy Clark : « Mary-Lou est une fille jeune et naïve qui vient d'une toute petite ville. Elle recherche l'amour et elle est instantanément attirée par le personnage fragile et se demande qui est Thomas Jerome Newton, parce qu'elle aussi est en manque, elle est seule. »

Roeg : « La plus ancienne question entre amants est "à quoi tu penses, chéri(e) ?" puis "à quoi tu penses vraiment ?" Mary-Lou et Newton se fréquentent depuis un moment mais, même si elle le trouve un peuétrange et décalé, elle n'a pas idée d'où il vient. Aussi quand elle lui promet qu'il peut tout lui dire, ce qui dans un contexte humain signifie "Tu peux tout me dire et je t'aimerai toujours", il lui montre qu'il est un extraterrestre et comment il fait l'amour – par un échange de fluides corporels. Bien sûr, elle prend peur. »

Nathan Bryce (Rip Torn) est devenu un professeur divorcé qui batifole avec ses étudiantes, jusqu'à ce qu'il commence ses recherches sur World Enterprises et Newton. Lorsque Newton et Bryce se rencontrent, une amitié se développe entre eux, et ils semblent dès le départ avoir un lien psychique. Avant leur première rencontre, Newton « entend » Bryce, et Newton apparaît même à Bryce comme un mirage alors qu'il est en train de pêcher. Mayersberg : « Nous voulions introduire la notion de perception extrasensorielle. Newton a plusieurs longueurs d'avance – il sait ce que Bryce pense. Newton sait qu'il va être démasqué et dit à Bryce : "Ne soyez pas suspicieux. N'ayez pas peur." L'histoire tient à ce que les autres font quand ils doivent intégrer le fait que Newton sait tout avant tout le monde. »

Bryce trahit la confiance de Newton en prenant secrètement une radio de son corps, qui révèle sa physiologie extraterrestre. Bowie : « Pour moi, le film reste une histoire de trahison sous des dehors de science-fiction. Le moment où Newton comprend que Bryce a pris les clichés rappelle l'histoire de Jésus qui sait qu'il sera trahi par Judas. Newton sait qu'il va être trahi. C'est assez évident. Simplement, il ne fait rien pour l'empêcher. »

Quand Newton est sur le point de repartir, après avoir testé son vaisseau, le gouvernement intervient et le kidnappe. Le chauffeur de Newton l'a vendu et Mary-Lou empoche de l'argent pour le quitter. Mayersberg : « En fait, tout le monde trahit Newton, parce que quand vous avez cette capacité, ce pouvoir, tout le monde veut obtenir quelque chose de vous. Ils veulent de l'argent. Quand l'agence gouvernementale vient jeter Farnsworth par la fenêtre, c'est seulement parce qu'il exerce un contrôle trop étroit sur l'entreprise. Le gouvernement veut contrôler le monde de la finance. Ce qui nous a intéressés, c'est l'idée qu'il n'y a pas de séparation entre les affaires et la politique, et je trouve que nous avons été plutôt prescients à ce propos. Il s'agit d'une entreprise qui prend d'assaut une autre entreprise – le fait qu'une de ces entreprises soit l'État est sans importance. »

Quant à Bryce, il s'installe ensuite avec Mary-Lou – sa façon de trahir. Clark : « Mary-Lou ne peut pas aimer pleinement Nathan Bryce parce qu'elle est toujours obsédée par Newton, si bien que leur relation est désynchronisée. Thomas Jerome Newton, lui, ne s'est jamais remis d'avoir laissé sa femme et ses enfants sur sa planète. Il est condamné à une quête de l'impossible qui le fait dépérir, tout comme Mary-Lou dépérit à ses côtés. Personne n'obtient ce qu'il veut. »

Rip Torn : « Le drame de la vie de Newton, c'est qu'il a échoué. Il n'a pas réussi à sauver sa culture. Il n'a pas réussi à sauver sa famille. C'est l'histoire de gens qui ont manqué le bateau, mais continuent à avancer. »

## PRODUCTION

Roeg a apporté le scénario, avec la promesse de Bowie, à différents studios de production, et a accepté l'offre de Michael Deeley chez British Lion. Bien que British Lion soit une maison ancienne, fondée en 1927 – qui compte notamment dans son catalogue *Le Troisième Homme* (1949), *Sa Majesté des Mouches* (1963) et *Le Dieu d'osier* (1973) – sa situation financière est précaire. Quand la Paramount, qui avait distribué avec succès le précédent film de Roeg *Ne vous retournez pas* (1973) aux États-Unis, accepta de payer 1,5 million de dollars pour les droits américains, British Lion réussit à obtenir un prêt de la banque, cautionné par ce partenariat. Contrairement au roman, le film contient des séquences qui se passent sur la planète natale de Newton, pour lesquelles la production recherchait un paysage aride. Ils avaient aussi besoin d'être proches d'un aéroport pour que les rushes soient envoyés à Los Angeles tous les jours, y soient développés et reviennent à Roeg, qui les visionnait. La production décida de se baser à Albuquerque, au Nouveau-Mexique. « Le Nouveau-Mexique est imprégné d'un certain mysticisme dont je n'avais jusqu'alors pas conscience, raconte Mayersberg. Il y a plus de témoignages sur des apparitions d'ovnis ou d'extraterrestres au Nouveau-Mexique que dans le reste du monde réuni. » C'est aussi au Nouveau-Mexique que se trouve la White Sands Test Facility (utilisée par la NASA et l'armée, qui y a notamment testé la première bombe nucléaire en 1945) et que s'est déroulé l'incident de Roswell, en 1947. Le producteur Michael Deeley voyait d'autres avantages à cette localisation : « C'était hors du champ de vision des syndicats du cinéma, et étant donné qu'à l'époque Albuquerque n'était pas une ville prospère, nous et notre argent y étions accueillis à bras ouverts. La ville possédait depuis peu un hôtel Hilton, qui hébergea l'équipe pour 15 dollars la nuit et nous laissa garer nos camions sur son parking. Si j'avais engagé une équipe à Hollywood, le coût aurait été prohibitif, impossible, alors on a décidé de faire ce pari. Chaque membre de l'équipe s'est présenté à l'ambassade américaine de Grosvenor Square, à Londres, et a déposé une demande individuelle de visa touristique. Nous avons privatisé un avion d'Aer Lingus dans lequel nous avons embarqué toute l'équipe et autant de matériel que possible, et nous nous sommes envolés pour Albuquerque. Deux jours plus tard, nous commencions à tourner. C'était la première fois – et probablement la dernière – qu'une équipe britannique au complet tournait un film entier en Amérique. »

« C'était ma première fois en Amérique, j'ai tout de suite aimé ce pays, que j'aime toujours », se souvient le photographe David James, exprimant un sentiment

NASA

largement partagé par le reste de l'équipe. Bowie et son ami Geoff MacCormack (fidèle acolyte de Bowie sous le nom de Warren Peace) ont pris le train depuis Los Angeles et ont séjourné au Hilton avec nous. James : « La majorité des Anglais étaient à l'hôtel, mais quelques-uns avaient loué des logements de leur côté. Nic aimait tourner à la lumière du matin, alors en général nous nous levions vers 6 heures / 6 h 30 et nous allions sur le plateau pour prendre le petit déjeuner. Nous avions un répertoire avec les coordonnées de tout le monde et la plupart avaient des voitures, alors nous allions sur les différents lieux de tournage par nos propres moyens. Le Nouveau-Mexique est magnifique le matin ; le ciel est très clair et le soleil encore bas. Il régnait une atmosphère communautaire et nous passions parfois le petit déjeuner à comparer nos gueules de bois. Nic et le chef op' [Anthony Richmond] finissaient par arriver et préparaient la scène du jour. Puis les acteurs se pointaient et commençaient à répéter. »

Les onze semaines de tournage commencèrent le lundi 2 juin 1975 à Los Lunas – dont Roeg trouvait que le nom (« Les Lunes ») était de bon augure – avec les scènes où Newton entre à Haneyville, vend une bague en or et boit de l'eau puisée dans le Rio Grande. James : « Nous ne perdions pas de temps. Nous nous mettions en place très vite. »

Newton entre dans la ville et passe à côté d'une fête foraine abandonnée, où un soulard l'apostrophe. Bowie : « La première chose en lien avec l'humain que Newton voit est l'effet produit par cet alcool qui va aussi le détruire, ou du moins l'empêcher de partir. » Ensuite une grosse bourrasque soulève une structure gonflable de la foire. Roeg : « Le ballon s'est détaché et a commencé à nous tomber dessus. Je leur ai dit de ne pas couper, de continuer à tourner. »

James : « Fats Domino est venu au Hilton avec son groupe et, grâce à David, Geoff MacCormack et moi avons pu avoir une place au premier rang. » Ce soir-là encore, on consomma beaucoup de Budweiser. Geoff MacCormack : « À neuf ans, David et moi avions acheté "Blueberry Hill", alors nous étions vraiment impatients de voir le grand homme sur scène. Après le concert nous avons trébuché jusqu'aux coulisses et frappé à la porte de sa loge. Une énorme voix a tonné depuis l'intérieur : "C'est qui ?" "David Bowie." "Qui ?" "David Bowie, de Londres." "David *qui* ?" » Des filles frappèrent à la porte et entrèrent tout de suite. Bowie réessaya. « La porte s'est ouverte, et là, devant nous, se dressait le plus immense homme noir que j'aie jamais vu. Il nous a informés que M. Domino était occupé pour l'instant, puis nous a refermé la porte au nez. David ne s'est pas senti insulté par l'épisode. Au contraire, c'était vraiment trop drôle. » James : « Ensuite nous sommes allés au café avec quelques musiciens du groupe, et Bowie s'est mis à danser sur les tables. Les serveuses lui criaient de descendre avant qu'elles n'appellent les flics. Et Bowie répondait : "Appelez-les. Appelez-les !" »

MacCormack : « Après quelque temps passé au Hilton, David a loué un petit ranch près de Santa Fe, et son assistante personnelle Coco [Schwab] et moi nous sommes installés avec lui. David a profité de la véranda lumineuse pour recommencer à peindre. » Entre deux scènes, Bowie écrivait des chansons et des nouvelles, notamment sa pseudo-autobiographie, *The Return of the Thin White Duke*.

L'hôtel Artesia, dans la ville du même nom, était un lieu clé. La majeure partie de l'établissement n'était pas utilisée, si bien que la production a eu la liberté d'abattre des cloisons et d'agencer les pièces à sa convenance. L'endroit a été utilisé pour l'arrivée de

Newton à l'hôtel, la scène de l'ascenseur et les scènes dans la chambre avec Mary-Lou, mais il a aussi servi de geôle lorsque le gouvernement arrête Newton.

James : « Nic créait un décor et y plaçait les personnages. C'était sa magie à lui. Ils répétaient. Ils lisaient les dialogues, et il y avait d'inévitables modifications. Ensuite Nic demandait aux acteurs de répéter la scène et réglait le placement des caméras. Il parlait d'une voix douce sur le plateau, toujours avec ce sens de l'humour anglais un peu pince-sans-rire. »

Clark : « David n'était pas du genre à exprimer ce qu'il ressentait, donc on ne savait jamais ce qui se passait dans sa tête. En plus, il restait le plus souvent avec son entourage. En dehors de nos scènes communes, nous n'avons jamais dîné tous les deux ou passé du temps ensemble hors plateau. Il était très réservé et calme, ce qui me convenait parfaitement, puisque mon personnage ne savait jamais ce qui se passait dans la tête de Thomas Newton. »

Bowie : « C'était la première fois que je faisais ça. J'ignorais tout de la procédure habituelle [dans le cinéma], alors j'agissais beaucoup à l'instinct, et mon instinct était plutôt dissolu. J'apprenais juste mon texte de la journée et je le jouais comme je le sentais. En fait, je me sentais tout aussi aliéné que ce personnage. C'était une performance plutôt naturelle pour moi…. une bonne exhibition de quelqu'un qui se désagrège littéralement devant vous. J'étais dans une insécurité totale, chargé d'environ 10 grammes [de cocaïne] par jour. Je suis resté complètement perché du début à la fin. »

Le chef décorateur Brian Eatwell a construit les extérieurs de la propriété de style japonais de Newton au bord du lac Fenton, à 130 kilomètres au nord d'Albuquerque dans les monts de Jemez, à l'ouest de Los Alamos où était basé le Manhattan

Project. (Les scènes à l'intérieur de la maison aux murs arrondis en adobe – pour que Newton ne se blesse pas – ont été filmées à Santa Fe.) De l'autre côté du lac, la cabane du garde forestier est devenue la maison de Nathan Bryce.

Le lac regorgeait de truites. James : « Rip Torn et moi aimions tous deux la pêche à la mouche. Un soir, alors que nous tournions sur le ponton en bois, au lac, après avoir rangé le matériel, quelques locaux ont allumé un feu de camp sur lequel ils ont mis de l'eau à bouillir. Rip nous a appris à pêcher les écrevisses ; on les attrapait, on les jetait dans la marmite et on les mangeait. »

Bowie : « J'adorais Rip – c'était un type merveilleux – il avait un faux air d'Hemingway ou de Mailer. Il était très viril dans ses manières. Pour Rip, chaque jour et chaque nuit représentaient une énorme aventure. Tous les matins, nous attendions le récit de ses exploits avec impatience. Il commençait : "Je vais vous dire, ce qui s'est passé hier soir…" Il escaladait des barbelés, on le retrouvait dans des fossés… »

« Un jour, Rip est arrivé sur le plateau d'une humeur particulièrement bougonne. Pour une raison ou une autre, il en voulait à Nic et il a grogné : "Si tu comptes me traiter comme un chien, alors je vais réagir comme un chien." Nic a levé les yeux sur lui, il a dit au cameraman : "On ne filmera pas M. Torn aujourd'hui." Et il l'a laissé en plan, fulminant. »

White Sands, près d'Alamogordo, fournit les décors pour le monde extraterrestre où évoluent Bowie, Clark et deux enfants acteurs, qui forment une famille extraterrestre. Ils portent des combinaisons moulantes enveloppées d'une sorte de toile de drains contenant l'eau si précieuse. La caractéristique physique prédominante des aliens est leurs yeux de chats. Bowie : « À l'époque les lentilles de contact étaient le plus

souvent en plastique rigide et elles faisaient vraiment, vraiment très mal aux yeux. J'étais très déshydraté et le désert n'arrangeait rien. » Roeg : « Quand Candy est allée se faire poser ses lentilles, la première s'est carrément collée à son œil. Elle était beaucoup trop ajustée. Il a fallu au docteur plus d'une heure pour trouver le moyen de l'enlever. »

Le film est parcouru de références visuelles et textuelles aux trains, qui, pour Newton, représentent ses adieux à sa famille. Pour visualiser cette scène dans le film, Brian Eatwell pose un rail sur le sol désertique et construit un train extraterrestre, avec une surface organique et des voiles solaires, autour d'un vieux tracteur. Bowie : « Quand le train a débarqué, ça ne ressemblait pas du tout à ce que Nic avait imaginé. Il est devenu tout bleu, puis rouge, puis blanc, et il a dit : "C'est quoi, ça ?" "C'est votre train, monsieur." "Ce n'est pas un train, c'est une putain de niche pour chien !" Mais il s'y est fait. » L'affaire se complique encore quand le tracteur tombe en panne. Comme il est impossible de changer les pièces, ils attachent le train à des câbles et le font tirer hors champ par des chevaux. James : « Ce genre de problème est normal sur un film. »

Après dix semaines de tournage au Nouveau-Mexique, la production déménage à Los Angeles pour les derniers jours. James : « Il a fallu qu'on travaille clandestinement à cause des syndicats locaux et des permis de travail. » Bowie loue une maison à Bel-Air et il enregistre aux studios Cherokee les jours où il ne tourne pas.

Chez Tower Records, sur le Sunset Strip, un Bryce vieilli achète un disque d'un certain Visiteur (alias Newton). On distingue aussi plusieurs exemplaires de l'album *Young Americans* de Bowie dans un bac à l'arrière-plan. Le spectacle de kabuki, que Newton quitte avant la fin parce que la violence le perturbe trop, est tourné dans un restaurant japonais, également sur Sunset. L'ultime rencontre entre Bryce et Newton est filmée au restaurant Butterfield's sur Sunset Boulevard. Roeg : « C'est un milieu tellement dirigé par l'argent qu'il encourage l'idée que tout doit forcément être linéaire. Dans la première scène, Newton longe un champ de fête foraine. Au moment où nous passions, un vieux clochard installé dans un des manèges s'est assis d'un bond et a lâché un rot. Il n'y avait aucun moyen de prévoir ça. Le premier bruit humain du film est un rot, et c'est aussi le dernier, quand Bowie rote à sa table. J'aime cette idée de hasard. Il faut regarder tout ce qui se passe autour de vous quand vous filmez. Ce qui fait rire Dieu, ce sont les gens qui font des projets. »

## POSTPRODUCTION

Roeg retourne au Royaume-Uni pour monter le film avec Graeme Clifford. Deeley : « Le projet initial était que David Bowie fournisse la musique du film ». Bowie : « J'ai passé deux ou trois mois à assembler des petits morceaux et des bribes. » Mais les compositions qu'il livre sont rejetées par Roeg. Paul Buckmaster, un violoncelliste qui avait fait les arrangements de « Space Oddity », a travaillé avec Bowie sur cette bande originale et explique pourquoi sa musique n'a pas été utilisée : « D'abord, ni la composition ni l'interprétation n'étaient au niveau qu'exige un bon film, ensuite je ne pense pas qu'elle convenait au film et pour finir, ce n'était pas vraiment ce que recherchait Nic Roeg. » Deeley : « Le monteur de Nic, Graeme Clifford, a ensuite voulu utiliser des titres de Pink Floyd, mais ils étaient impossibles à obtenir et auraient dans tous les

cas été trop chers. Au bout du compte, John Phillips, ex-membre de The Mamas and the Papas, a combiné des nouveaux thèmes musicaux avec des morceaux existants. » Phillips a entendu les compositions de Bowie, qu'il décrira plus tard comme « obsédantes et magnifiques, avec des carillons, des cloches japonaises, et ce qui sonnait comme des bruitages électroniques de vent et de vagues ». Cette description peut aussi s'appliquer aux six morceaux du compositeur de rock progressif japonais Stomu Yamashta qui ont été utilisés à des moments clés du film. Quant à la bande originale proposée par Bowie, elle n'a pas été totalement perdue. « Certains titres figurent sur *Station to Station*, explique Bowie, mais une autre partie est devenue l'album *Low*, que j'ai réalisé avec Brian Eno à Berlin quelques années plus tard. »

Deeley : « Pendant que la musique était péniblement posée sur les images, j'ai fait un aller-retour à New York pour montrer le film au nouveau président de Paramount Pictures, Barry Diller. Ce visionnage devait enclencher le premier paiement de Paramount en vertu du contrat signé avec British Lion. Les lumières se sont rallumées et Diller est resté muet pendant plusieurs minutes. Puis il a fini par dire : "Ce n'est pas le film que la Paramount a acheté. Le film que nous avons acheté est linéaire et celui-ci ne l'est pas." Il nous a ensuite exprimé son embarras à honorer un accord conclu par son entreprise avant son entrée en fonction. C'était un désastre pour British Lion. Aucun autre grand distributeur américain n'accepterait de récupérer *L'Homme qui venait d'ailleurs* dans ces conditions, le projet était comme souillé par le rejet de la Paramount. Hollywood est extrêmement superstitieux. »

C'est finalement Don Rugoff, de Cinema V, qui paye une avance de 850 000 dollars pour sa sortie américaine.

## SORTIE

La première de *L'Homme qui venait d'ailleurs* a lieu au Leicester Square Theatre de Londres le 18 mars 1976. L'accueil de la critique est mitigé. Roeg : « Un des critiques s'est plaint de la phrase "Tout commence et finit dans l'éternité" Je lui ai dit : "Vous êtes au courant que c'est du [William] Blake ?" » Les différents axes de l'intrigue, les motifs visuels récurrents et les thèmes qui soudent le film sont difficiles à percevoir dès le premier visionnage en raison du montage elliptique. Roeg a modifié la syntaxe cinématographique en effaçant l'emprise temporelle, à laquelle le public s'accroche en général : « Je trouve que le film se rapproche plutôt d'une existence menée par à-coups. C'est dur de discerner la vraie histoire des gens à la fin de leur vie. » Roeg veut que les spectateurs « lisent l'écran » et laissent le film « œuvrer sur eux ».

Cinema V sort le film en Amérique le 28 mai, mais ils exercent leur droit contractuel de modifier le montage et raccourcissent le film de 20 minutes – Roeg en est « dévasté et affligé ». La critique se montre tout aussi mitigée.

Au fil des quarante dernières années, le film a gagné en stature, en grande partie parce que la nouvelle grammaire adoptée par Roeg pour la première fois sur *L'Homme qui venait d'ailleurs* a été reprise par d'autres réalisateurs et que le public a appris à « lire l'écran ». Bowie : « Je nourrissais déjà un certain goût pour la fragmentation parce que j'étais fan des découpages de William S. Burroughs. Nic avait compris que deux éléments qui se percutent peuvent produire un troisième élément d'information dont personne n'avait conscience et il était enchanté quand il voyait ces coïncidences faire sens, un ordre naître du chaos. L'ordre dans le chaos est aujourd'hui une théorie

twenty-ten-wilshire-bldg
DATSUN
2007

scientifique éprouvée. Je me suis saisi de cet élément et je l'ai beaucoup utilisé dans mon travail ultérieur, et j'imagine que cette démarche a atteint son apogée dans ma collaboration avec Brian Eno. Mon travail s'est certainement nourri de la notion de coïncidence et du procédé de fragmentation que j'ai appris à connaître sur ce film avec Nic. »

À la fin du film, Bryce retrouve la trace de Newton grâce à un disque de « poésie et de musique comme vous n'en avez jamais entendu », du Visiteur. « Vous avez aimé ? » demande Newton. « Pas trop », réplique Bryce. « Bien, dit Newton. De toute façon je ne l'ai pas fait pour vous. » Newton espère que son œuvre passera à la radio et qu'elle atteindra un jour la famille qu'il a laissée derrière lui. Roeg a compris le réel drame de la situation, sans doute à la racine du mal dont souffre Newton : « Il n'est plus un visiteur, mais l'un d'entre nous. »

All images were supplied by Studiocanal. We would also like to thank the following: British Film Institute, Posters and Designs, London: Front Cover, 2/3, 6/7, 8/9, 12/13, 18, 26/27, 36/37, 62, 126/127, 142/143, 172/173, 185, 186, 196, 197, 218/219, 238/239, 260/261, 262/263, 268/269 (2), 289, 310/311, 314/315, 346/347, 430/431, 439
The Kobal Collection, London/New York: 236/237, 240/241

The editor would like to thank Massimo Moretti of Studiocanal for his enthusiastic participation and help in the making of this book, as well as photographer David James, who kindly spent two days in a Pinewood archive, looking through the original negatives and reminiscing about his on- and off-set experiences.



© 2024 TASCHEN GmbH
Hohenzollernring 53, 50672 Köln
www.taschen.com

Editor
Paul Duncan/Wordsmith Solutions

German Translation
Thomas J. Kinne, Nauheim

French Translation
Alice Pétillot, Bordeaux

Printed in Bosnia-Herzegovina
ISBN 978-3-8365-9316-8